THE OFFICIAL BASEBALL HALL OF FAME ANSWER BOOK

Mark Alvarez

LITTLE SIMON
Published by Simon & Schuster Inc.
New York

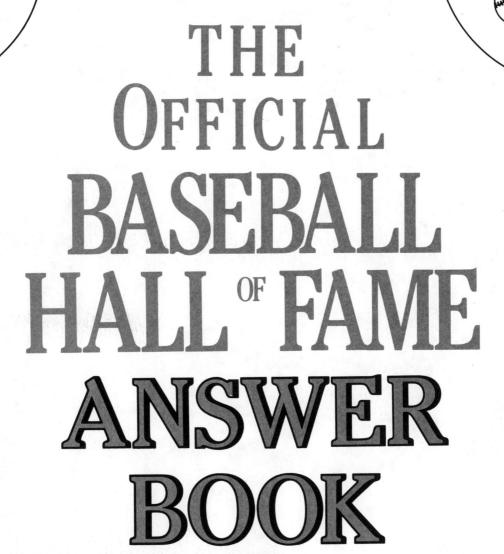

A BASEBALL INK BOOK

LITTLE SIMON
Simon & Schuster Building
Rockefeller Center
1230 Avenue of the Americas
New York, New York 10020
Copyright © 1989 by Professional Ink, Inc.
All rights reserved
including the right of reproduction
in whole or in part in any form.
LITTLE SIMON and colophon are trademarks
of Simon & Schuster Inc.
Manufactured in the United States of America
10 9 8 7 6 5 4 3 2 1
ISBN 0-671-67377-7

Photos courtesy of the National Baseball Library, Cooperstown, NY.

⚾ Contents ⚾

⚾ Who was the greatest ⚾ hitter in baseball history?

When I was a boy and I asked this question, the answer I always got was, "Ty Cobb." And when I looked in the record books, that choice seemed obvious. After all, the Georgia Peach had the highest lifetime batting average of anyone who ever played the game—.367. The great Detroit Tiger center fielder played from 1905 through 1928. In a thirteen-year span (1907–19) he won an amazing twelve American League batting championships—nine of them in a row (and batted .371 in his "off" year).

Many old-timers thought that Cobb was almost superhuman. There is a story that illustrates this in a humorous way. About 1960, the old outfielder Lefty O'Doul was asked at a banquet how he thought Cobb would have hit against modern pitching. "Oh, about .340," O'Doul said. The audience was shocked. Why such a "low" average under modern conditions that should make hitting easier? "Well, you have to remember," O'Doul replied, "that Mr. Cobb is over seventy years old."

When my elders got going on the topic of great hitters, three other names always seemed to come up too. Rogers Hornsby's .358 is the second-highest career batting average in history. He hit over .400 in three of four years in a row during the 1920s, and the baseball books I read were always calling him "baseball's greatest right-handed hitter" (Cobb batted left-handed).

Similarly, Shoeless Joe Jackson was always "baseball's greatest natural hitter." He batted .408 in his first full season in the big leagues and built a lifetime average of .356 before he was banned from the game for his part in the Black Sox Scandal of 1919. Jackson was a free-swinger in an era when most players slapped at the ball, and Babe Ruth used to say that he copied his batting style from Jackson's.

Ruth, himself, was the third man. The Babe is still probably the most famous baseball player who ever lived, and when I was a kid, his 714 lifetime home runs seemed to be a record no one would even approach, let alone surpass, as Hank Aaron did. But still, Cobb's .367 was much better than Ruth's lifetime .342, and most of the older fans I knew focused on that batting average and called Cobb the best hitter and Ruth the greatest slugger.

These days, people interested in the question of baseball's greatest hitter have begun to look at a lot more than a player's batting average. In simple terms, they figure things this way:

1. For a team to win, it has to score more runs than its opponent.
2. The only way for a team to score runs is to create them while it is at bat.
3. A batter's job is to help to create those runs.
4. The best batters are the ones who produce the most runs, either by batting them in or by scoring them.

Modern students of the game have come up with formulas to measure the value of hitters—even hitters of different eras who played under very different conditions. Some of these formulas look like a bad dream from algebra class, and different people have developed different equations. But all of them, no matter how much they jiggle the raw data of hits, runs, RBIs and the like, seem to point to one of two conclusions: the best hitter in baseball history—that is, the hitter who was best at producing runs for his team—was either Babe Ruth or Ted Williams, the great Red Sox slugger who played from 1939 through 1960.

This isn't too surprising, because the two men both combined high lifetime batting averages (.342 for Ruth, .344 for Williams) with great power (714 home runs for Ruth, 521 for Williams during a career in which he lost almost five prime years to the Marines). So they were both on base a lot, to be driven in by teammates, and they both knocked in a tremendous number of runs with their slugging.

Now, Cobb was no slouch as a run producer—he had 144 RBIs in 1911, and he still holds the all-time record for runs scored, but he played most of his career in an era when power hitting wasn't as highly valued as it is today, and when the home run—or even swinging hard from the end of the bat—was relatively rare. Some studies still place him as high as third on the list of all-time great hitters, ahead of greats like Hank Aaron, Stan Musial, and Lou Gehrig. Some place him much lower. But the top two spots al-

Ted Williams—the last man to bat .400; he hit for an average of .406 in 1941.

6

ways seem to belong to Williams and Ruth, Ruth and Williams.

If you're interested in getting a better idea of just what these mathematical analyses are like—and how you can apply them to your favorite active players—there are a number of books you can read to find out more about them. Try Bill James's *Historical Abstract*, along with his annual *Baseball Abstract*. Find a copy of *The Hidden Game of Baseball* by John Thorn and Pete Palmer. You should also consider joining the Society for American Baseball Research, known as SABR, which puts out a whole range of interesting publications every year. You can get information about SABR by writing to: Lloyd Johnson, Executive Director, P.O. Box 10033, Kansas City, MO 64111.

Oh, you want a definite answer to your question? I was hoping you'd be satisfied with my waffle. Okay. It's a tough call, and you'll find plenty of people to disagree with me, but I think the greatest hitter in baseball history was Ted Williams.

⚾ *What is the hardest position to play?* ⚾

There's no doubt in my mind that—for a youngster, at least—the hardest position is catcher. You have to wear that heavy, hot gear; squat down close behind another kid waving a heavy stick; leap or collapse to keep wild pitches from getting by you; and make that long, long throw to second base on steal attempts. You have to try to keep your eye on the ball while the batter swings; you have to learn how to chase foul pop-ups that seem to come out of the sky at crazy angles; and you have to do all this while you take lumps and bumps from foul tips and runners trying to score.

What I remember best from my days as a young catcher is the leathery smell of the mask, and the mud that would form on my face when the dirty padding came into contact with my sweaty cheeks and forehead. Catching was hard work in a way no other position could match.

But catching isn't the position that takes the most *skill*; shortstop is. Especially as players get into their mid-teens, you'll notice that the best athletes tend to gravitate to short. This is because shortstops have to be fast enough to go get a ball deep in the hole, and agile enough to make the double play while avoiding runners who try to knock them over. They also must have strong arms, so that once they chase down that ball way over toward third base, they can get it to first in time to beat the runner.

Shortstops are also supposed to be leaders on the field. It's the shortstop, for example, who signals the second baseman as to which of them will cover the bag on a steal attempt. And because they are leaders, shortstops have to have great baseball instincts. They have to know, without thinking, about what every other player on the field should be doing under certain circumstances: Cut-offs and backing up and throwing to the right base. You'll often hear shortstops praised as *smart* players.

Because their defense is so important, shortstops are quite often the worst hitters on a big-league team. Managers need their first basemen and outfielders to be strong hitters, but they're willing to pencil into the lineup day after day a weak hitter who has mastered the difficult art of playing short. A good example is Mark Belanger, who was the best shortstop in the American League during the 1970s. He turned in averages like .218, .206, and .213, but manager Earl Weaver was happy to have him in the lineup because he was so good with the glove.

There have been some great hitting players at the position, of course. Honus Wagner won eight National League batting championships while he played short for the Pirates in the early years of this century. Joe Cronin was a great slugger for the Senators and the Red Sox during the '20s and '30s. Ernie Banks was a shortstop when he was popping forty or more homers a year and winning two consecutive Most Valuable Player awards for the Cubs during the '50s. Today Cal Ripken, Jr., and Alan Trammell carry on in this hard-hitting tradition. Ozzie Smith, maybe the greatest *fielding* shortstop of all, doesn't hit many home runs, but he's become an excellent hitter who gets on base a lot. Managers love having such powerful bats in the lineup, but if these men weren't also great with the glove, they'd be moved to a less demanding position.

So. Which is the hardest position to play? Let's put it this way: catcher is the most work, but shortstop is the toughest to master.

Why do ballplayers wear those funny socks?

They *are* sort of strange when you think about it, aren't they? Baseball players wear two pairs of socks. Their woolen- or synthetic-blend stirrup socks are worn over a pair of long, thin white cotton socks known as "sanitary hose." These days, the fashion is to wear stirrups so high that the colored socks themselves become invisible. A few years back, you would have seen some socks that were solid-colored and some that were striped. Where did this two-pair arrangement originate? Why the term *sanitary hose*?

Well, in the old days, players wore long woolen stockings, much like the ones your grandfather probably wore with his knickers when he was a little boy.

In 1905, Napoleon Lajoie, the slugging second baseman who was the American League's first big star, was spiked in the foot. Dye from his blue stock-

Did Nap Lajoie's spike wound lead to stirrup socks?

8

ings got into the cut and gave Lajoie a serious case of blood poisoning, which made him pretty sick and kept him out of the lineup for most of the rest of the season.

A Rhode Island newspaperman named Jim Murphy has recently written a biography of Lajoie, and he thinks that it was after Nap's injury and illness that undyed white undersocks were adopted.

This makes sense, because if you look at old pictures, it's in the last half of the first decade of this century that you begin to see stirrup socks—with very low stirrups—being worn.

The fact that the white undersocks were meant to protect players from infection and blood poisoning accounts for the term *sanitary hose.*

⚾ *Who gives teams their names?* ⚾

In the early days, team nicknames were less important than they are today. Well into the 1930s, for example, many teams hadn't *officially* adopted a nickname, leaving that sort of thing to the often shifting whims of the press and the fans. Long ago, teams were frequently identified by city and league only: "the Boston Americans" or "the Philadelphia Nationals," for example.

But nicknames, formal or otherwise, have always existed. They often simply evolved from the color of the clubs' uniform trimmings. The Cincinnati Reds were originally called the Red Stockings because they wore red socks. The St. Louis Browns were togged out in uniforms with brown socks and accents. And the Cardinals are named after a color, not a bird. Even the Tigers got their name from the orange-and-black striped socks they wore.

Sometimes nicknames moved from one city to another. The original Boston team in the National Association (the major league of the era 1871–75) was quickly christened the Red Stockings, not so much because of the team's choice of uniform colors but because Manager Harry Wright had come to Boston from Cincinnati and had

brought most of his team with him. Since the new Boston squad was made up largely of Cincinnati players, fans and the press simply called the team after the players who constituted it: the Red Stockings.

The saga of the red socks has one more chapter. Boston's National Association team joined the National League when it was founded in 1876. Although it was sometimes called the Beaneaters over the next twenty-five years or so, it was also still generally known as the Red Stockings during the late 1890s. But when the American League invaded Boston in 1901, many Red Stockings players jumped to the new team in town. Once again, the nickname followed the players, and the new team, originally tagged the Pilgrims, inevitably took on the ancient name, this time shortened to the familiar Red Sox.

Names came about in other ways too. In Cleveland, the original American Association team of the 1880s was called the Forest Citys, because Cleveland was known as the Forest City. They got another nickname when a team official called a collection of angular, gangly team members Spiders. And the Cleveland Spiders remained as a National

League team through most of the 1890s. In the late '90s they got a Native American player named Louis Sockalexis. Sockalexis was a spectacular outfielder and hitter whose career was swiftly ruined by drink, but for a short while the sportswriters occasionally referred to the whole team as the Indians. By the time Cleveland had one of the worst seasons in baseball history (20–134 in 1899), the team was once again known as the Spiders. The club was dropped from the National League after that season, but Cleveland returned to the major leagues with an American League franchise in 1901. It was generally known, for the usual reasons, as the Blues. Then for a while it was called the Bronchos. In 1903, Napoleon Lajoie joined the team and excited the fans so much that when a Cleveland paper ran a contest to name the club, the winning title was the Naps.

It wasn't until the teens, with Lajoie fading and then gone, that fans and sportswriters, looking for a nickname that made sense and projected a good image, reached back into the club's history and once again began calling the team the Indians.

The Brooklyn team was known in the late 1880s as the Bridegrooms because several of its players were married at more or less the same time. Later, Brooklyn was dubbed the Trolley Dodgers because of the need, when in Brooklyn, to watch out for the trolleys that seemed to be all over the borough's streets at the turn of the century. The team was known for a while in the twenties as the Robins, after their rotund and eccentric manager Wilbert Robinson, Uncle Robbie. Sportswriters settled on the Dodgers for good after Robinson retired.

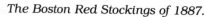

The Boston Red Stockings of 1887.

Pittsburgh got its nickname when the team signed a second baseman named Louis Bierbauer in 1891. His previous team, the Philadelphia club of the American Association, had failed to put Bierbauer on its reserve list, so Pittsburgh's action was legal. It was resented, though, and the club was called the Pirates for stealing Bierbauer away. The nickname stuck.

So nicknames have come from everywhere: uniform colors, favorite players or managers, strange events or situations and public contests—which are by far the most common way of naming new teams today. If you're interested in finding out more about team nicknames, look for a book called *Name That Team!* by Mike Lessiter.

⚾ *Who invented baseball?* ⚾

The pleasant legend that baseball was invented in 1839 by Abner Doubleday in a meadow at Cooperstown, New York, is unfortunately impossible to prove. Doubleday, who became a famous Civil War general, was at the United States Military Academy at West Point during the summer of 1839. In later life, he never spoke of "inventing" baseball, and when he died in 1893, his obituary said nothing about the game.

The story was put forward in 1907 by a committee called the Mills Commission, which wanted very badly to find a solidly American beginning for the game that had become our national pastime. The commission looked at many "letters and manuscripts . . . bearing upon the question of the origin of Base Ball," and found one from an old man named Abner Graves, who had been brought up in Cooperstown, New York. Graves said he had been present as a small boy on a day in 1839 when Abner Doubleday had scratched the shape of a diamond in the dirt and told the players where to position themselves. The Mills Commission decided that Graves had witnessed the "invention" of baseball and declared Abner Doubleday the inventor of the game.

According to Tom Heitz, the librarian at the Hall of Fame, there was an Abner Doubleday living in Cooperstown in 1839, a younger cousin to the Abner named by the Mills Commission. Heitz thinks that old Abner Graves might have confused the two. But Heitz says there's no reason to think that the younger Doubleday played anything but Town Ball, a version of the game that had been played all over the country under various rules for decades. Whatever the Doubleday role in baseball's beginnings—if any—the Hall of Fame is located in Cooperstown because baseball traces its roots to a similar rural atmosphere, and the village of Cooperstown, besides being a lovely home for baseball's traditions, is certainly an appropriate symbolic site.

Baseball actually wasn't invented. It evolved. Games with bats and balls were known thousands of years ago and were played in the Egypt of the Pharaohs. The English had been playing rounders for years, and cricket for even longer. In this country, games like "one old cat" had been played by youngsters for a long time, and the grown-ups had the game that was sometimes called Round Ball and sometimes called Town Ball. But

11

Alexander Cartwright, in about 1848.

baseball *was* codified, and there is a man who is generally credited with setting down the basic rules of the game as we now know it.

Alexander Cartwright was a member of the Knickerbocker Base Ball Club in New York. He and his friends met often to play a version of Town Ball probably not too different from what was being played in Cooperstown pastures at the time. One day, Cartwright showed up with a diagram and a list of rules that would make the game less rough and more regular—more suitable for a group of young gentlemen. Among other things, he eliminated the practice of hitting the runner with a thrown ball to get him out, a technique known as "soaking." His friends liked his ideas, and they caught on. The game he spelled out is recognizably baseball, although few of his rules and regulations exist in their original form any longer. Although it would be wrong to call Cartwright baseball's inventor, he is today generally given most of the credit once reserved for Abner Doubleday. But remember, baseball did not spring to life in a single idea by either man—it just grew.

If you want to read more about the game's evolution, there are two good books to check: Robert Henderson's *Ball, Bat and Bishop* (Rockport Press, 1947) and Harold Peterson's *The Man Who Invented Baseball* (Scribners, 1973).

⚾ Why do first basemen ⚾ wear mitts instead of gloves?

Think about it for a minute. The only two people on a team who are allowed to wear mitts (gloves without individual fingers) are the two players who catch thrown balls more often than batted balls: the first baseman and the catcher. Many of these thrown balls are coming as fast as the pitcher or infielder can fire them. Mitts developed simply as hand protection.

The catcher's mitt came along first. Receivers began by stuffing padding between two pairs of the little gloves, often with their fingers chopped off, that some players wore in the 1870s and 1880s. Real mitts made their appearance shortly thereafter. The great catcher Buck Ewing, who played for the Giants in the 1880s and 1890s, wore what was considered an enormous mitt that grew even bigger as he kept adding layers of padding. First basemen were quick to pick up on the benefits of padded mitts, and they were wearing them by the mid-1890s.

For a while, players at other positions were allowed to wear mitts too. I've seen a photo of John McGraw playing third base for the Baltimore Orioles of the 1890s wearing what looks like a first baseman's mitt. I'm not sure, but I think that what players at positions other than catcher and first base liked about the mitts was more their size than their padding. A bigger piece of leather let them reach and hang on to more ground balls. This was considered an outrage. Many people thought that letting infielders use the mitts took the skill out of the game, and a rule was soon passed making the big mitts legal only for first basemen and catchers. The other players went back to their little gloves.

John McGraw, Oriole third baseman and later Giant manager.

Today, neither catchers nor first basemen use their mitts mainly for padding. While catchers especially still need protection against 90-mile-an-hour fastballs, most balls are caught in the webbing of the big, hinged modern mitts, not in their palms.

And these days, the fielder's glove is a much better tool for general defensive chores than any mitt. No infielder today would even think of using a catcher's or first baseman's mitt. In fact, fielders' gloves have gotten so big and so flexible that I've often wondered why outfielders who are converted to first base bother learning to play with a mitt.

⚾ Who was the greatest player of all time? ⚾

Well, this is probably baseball's most often asked and debated question. Over the years, many people who've known an awful lot about the game have come up with many different answers. Let's take a look at some of them.

Nineteenth-century players always get the short end of the stick when greatness is debated. Precious few people alive today were even little children when these men played, and records were less carefully kept ninety and a hundred years ago than they are today. But as late as the 1920s, after everybody knew how good players like Ty Cobb and Honus Wagner and Babe Ruth were, there were men around who claimed that the best they'd ever seen was Buck Ewing, who made his name with the New York Giants.

Ewing was a catcher, although he played a fair number of games at first base and in the outfield, and a few at second and short. He even pitched a few times. It is said that he had an arm so good that as a catcher he could rifle the ball to second base on a line without even coming out of his crouch. As you can see with a quick look in Macmillan's *Baseball Encyclopedia*, Ewing's statistics are very good, but they don't seem to support the proposition that he was the greatest ballplayer who ever lived. He clearly had good power for his day, and he ran well, but there must have been more to his game than his statistics show. Many men who saw him play, or played with or against him, called him the best all-around player they'd ever seen.

The other nineteenth-century name that sometimes comes up in this discussion is Adrian "Cap" Anson, who played first base for the Chicago White Stockings for twenty-two years and was baseball's first 3,000-hit man. He and Ewing were the first nineteenth-century players elected to the Hall of Fame. But I don't think Anson was even the best first baseman of his time (check the record on Dan Brouthers and see if you don't agree), let alone the best player ever.

There's one more old-timer I really should mention. Mike "King" Kelly was probably the most famous player of the nineteenth century. He had a popular song—"Slide, Kelly, Slide"—written about him, and he was sold by Chicago to Boston for $10,000, which in 1887 was a tremendous amount of money. Kelly was a fine player, who led the league in batting and runs scored a few times. He was especially well-known for

14

his daring baserunning, and his "Kelly Spread" was an early version of the hook slide.

He was also something of a lovable rogue, who was not above breaking the rules of the game if there was an advantage in it for his club. There are all kinds of old stories about his cutting directly from second base, through the pitcher's box to home plate, while the single umpire who ran the games in those days was looking in the other direction. Kelly can't seriously be considered as baseball's greatest player, but he wasn't called King for nothing. He was certainly one of the game's great all-time personalities.

On to the twentieth century. The battle here always seems to be between Ty Cobb, the tough, high-average hitter and slashing baserunner of the dead-ball era, and Babe Ruth, the great lively ball slugger. Not so fast, though. There are a few other men who have to be considered. First comes Honus Wagner, the Pittsburgh Pirate who is still generally considered the greatest shortstop in baseball history. Because shortstop is the key defensive position, any man who can lay claim to that title has a serious claim to the whole shebang.

Wagner came up to the big leagues eight years before Cobb, but they were both playing great baseball at the same time, during the first decade of this century. American Leaguer Cobb usually hit for a higher average, but Wagner won eight National League batting championships himself, while compiling a .329 lifetime average. Cobb was the greatest baserunner of his time, but Wagner also led his league in stolen bases five times. The two men met in the 1909 World Series, a showcase in which Wagner clearly outplayed his Tiger rival. Many baseball men at the time and in later years said over and over that Wagner was baseball's greatest player—better than Cobb, better than anybody. Now, Wagner was a pleasant man, a much more popular figure than Cobb, who was very difficult to get along with. So some of those judgments may have been based at least partly on personality rather than on talent. But Wagner had the talent. He's a serious contender.

I once interviewed a great old Red Sox pitcher named Smokey Joe Wood. He said to me, "Cobb was the greatest player who ever lived. . . . If there'd been a higher league, he'd have been the only one in it." Many players and fans felt that way. Cobb was an obnoxious, aggressive man who was driven to be the best, and he dominated the American League for well over a decade. He won twelve batting titles; nine in a row. He stole 96 bases in 1915, a record that stood for almost half a century. He was the first (and until Pete Rose came along, the only) man to collect 4,000 hits. He played more games, scored more runs, and collected more total bases than anyone else of his era. He is still at, or very close to, the top of the all-time list in most of the important offensive categories. In his time and for a long while afterward, Cobb was considered by the mass of fans to be the greatest player ever. Many people *still* think he was.

This brings us to Ruth. The Babe started his professional career as a pitcher, and he wasn't just a good one; he was a great one. In 1915, 1916, and 1917, the three years before he started playing a lot of outfield, Ruth was 65–33, for a very high winning percentage of .663. He led the American League in Earned Run Average and shutouts one year, and in complete games another. He set a World Series record for consecutive scoreless innings. He would have been a great star even if he'd never picked up a bat.

But, of course, Babe Ruth did pick up a bat, and when he did, he changed the

The Babe.

game. By 1918, he was only a part-time pitcher because he was playing in the outfield so much. The next year, still pitching in seventeen games, he set a new season's record with 29 home runs—a tremendous number in 1919.

But it was in 1920, after he'd been traded from the Boston Red Sox to the New York Yankees, that the Babe really exploded. His 54 home runs that year were more than all but one other *full team* in baseball could match. Ruth just went on from there, eventually leading the league in home runs twelve times, in RBIs six times, and in slugging average thirteen times. Fans loved to watch the Babe, and they came in droves to see him. Other players began going for the long ball. The old way of playing ball—scratching for a run at a time—was on the way out. Ruth made the home run the most highly prized play in baseball. And it's stayed that way.

There have been many great players since Ruth: Lou Gehrig, Joe DiMaggio, Ted Williams, Stan Musial, Henry Aaron. But the one you most often hear compared to Cobb and Ruth as the greatest of all time is Willie Mays of the Giants. Just the other day I heard a well-known broadcaster say something like this: "Mays was the best I ever saw. I don't see how anyone could ever have been better." Players who played with or against Willie are always saying things like that about him.

In a way, Mays combined the skills of Ruth and Cobb. He was a great baserunner who led the National League in stolen bases four times. He was also a terrific hitter who led the league in average once, and in home runs four times. On top of this, he was a great center fielder—a much better outfielder than either Cobb or Ruth. Mays was also exciting. Like Cobb and Ruth and precious few others, he added electricity to a game just by being in the lineup.

So who is it? Who's the greatest player of all time? Maury Allen wrote a book a few years ago called *Baseball's 100*, in which he picks his top hundred players. His choice for number one is Mays. John Thorn and Pete Palmer make a strong statistical case in *The Hidden Game of Baseball* that Ruth was the greatest—by far. About six zillion books and articles I read when I was a kid agreed that Cobb was the man.

I think Thorn and Palmer (and a few million other people) are right. The numbers show that Babe Ruth was one of the two greatest hitters who ever swung a bat. He was also a great pitcher. And he fundamentally changed the way the game was played. Put it all together and I think that qualifies him as the greatest. But I wouldn't toss any of these other guys off my team!

⚾ *How did the World Series get started?* ⚾

The Series has been around a while. In fact, the first contests billed as World Series were held way back in the 1880s, between the champions of the National League and the American Association, which was then a major league. These matchups were much less formal than the Series is today. For one thing, they were arranged between the teams themselves, not their leagues. The owners just got together and agreed on the number of games to be played (one Series of the era went fifteen games), where the teams would meet (not necessarily the home park of either team), and how the gate receipts would be divided between winner and loser.

The most famous World Series of the 1880s was held in 1886, between the St. Louis Browns of the American Association and the Chicago White Stockings of the National League. To add a little interest, the owners agreed that it would be a winner-take-all contest—the losing players would take home no money. The Browns won it when Curt Welch stole home in the bottom of the tenth inning of the sixth game. Welch's theft was immediately dubbed "the $15,000 slide," because it guaranteed that he and his teammates would split the total gate receipts. (Actually, the Series took in a little over a thousand dollars less than that, but who's going to call it "the $13,910.20 slide"?)

The last of these old World Series was held in 1890. The American Association was already in pretty bad shape, and it folded after the 1891 season. There was no longer another league for the National League's champion to play at the end of the regular season.

The best team still got some recogni-tion, though. Starting in 1887, actress Helen Dauvray had presented the Dau-vray Cup to baseball's best team—the winner of the World Series—and she continued to hand it over to the National League pennant winner through 1893. The cup disappeared on its way to Kansas City that year, where it was sup-posed to be awarded to the barnstorm-ing Boston Beaneaters. Miss Dauvray, whose marriage to John Montgomery Ward of the New York Giants had ended in divorce, probably decided she'd had enough of the game. The trophy was not replaced.

In 1894, William C. Temple of Pitts-burgh picked up the slack by offer-ing the Temple Cup to the winner of a postseason series between the first-

Boston's Huntington Avenue Grounds in 1903, just before the final game of the first modern World Series.

18

and second-place teams in the National League. The Temple Cup Series lasted four years, but fans just didn't seem to care about it. They figured that the pennant-winner was the real champ, and that what happened in a short series with the second-place team just didn't matter that much. So from 1898 until 1903, there was no postseason championship series and no special trophy for the best team in the game.

What is usually called the first "modern" World Series was held in 1903, when the American League Boston Pilgrims beat the National League Pittsburgh Pirates. It's true that this was the first Series between the American and National League champions, but the arrangements were much like those made between the American Association and National League champi-

ons during the 1880s. There was no formal agreement between the leagues. The owners just got together and agreed on terms. In fact, the next year, there was no Series, because John McGraw of the National League Champion New York Giants hated American League President Ban Johnson, and simply refused to let his team play against the champions of what he called "a minor league."

But the fans had enjoyed the 1903 Series, wanted more, and most owners realized a regular postseason competition would be good for the game. So in 1905, the two leagues got together and formally decided to have a World Series between league champions every year. The Series was quickly established as America's most important and most popular sporting event, and it has remained so ever since.

⚾ You keep mentioning "modern" ⚾ baseball. When did modern baseball start?

Good question. Baseball's modern era is usually dated from 1901, the year the American League set itself up in competition with the National League as a second major league. But I think there are two other dates that could just as reasonably be considered the beginning of the "modern" game. It all depends on how you see things.

The first date is 1893. Before then, batters had to face a pitcher throwing from only fifty feet away. In that year, though, the pitching distance was set back to sixty feet, six inches, where it remains today. The game has changed in many ways since 1893, but nothing as basic as the distance between batter and pitcher has been touched. The diamond was set and—in a way, at least—so was the game.

The other date is twenty-seven years later: 1920. This was the year Babe Ruth hit 54 home runs. The lively ball had arrived, and from that point on, slugging became the focal point of the game. In most ways, the game today is more similar to the baseball of, say 1927, than baseball in 1927 was to the old-fashioned "dead-ball" game of ten or fifteen years before.

See what I mean? It all depends on how you see things. Most people use that 1901 date. But Macmillan's *Baseball Encyclopedia* makes no distinction between "modern" and "premodern" when it calculates the batting and fielding records of the game, and it separates pitching records at the 1893 point.

Why are the leaders of baseball teams called managers when in other sports they're called coaches?

In the beginning, baseball teams were usually run on the field by their captains—what today we would call playing managers. Professional teams had managers, but they usually weren't baseball players, and they generally took care of matters *off* the playing field—travel arrangements, business matters, and stuff like that.

Gradually, though, managers began to displace captains as the men who told the players what to do. I'm not sure, but I think this started when some captains got too old to play but still wanted to run their teams. They moved the old-style, non-ballplayers out of the managers' jobs, continued to take care of many business functions, but also kept control on the field.

By the turn of the century, the term *manager* had come to mean the man directing the team. Playing managers remained quite common, but many teams already had leaders who never swung a bat.

Unlike baseball, games like football and basketball didn't develop early on as professional sports. They originally got popular as pastimes for college and high-school-age kids. In many cases, the adult running the show had to do a lot of teaching—he had to *coach* his young players in the fine points of the game. Eventually, the title carried over into the big-time versions of the sports.

Who were the Black Sox?

The Black Sox were the White Sox. More precisely, the Black Sox were eight White Sox players who were accused of throwing the 1919 World Series to the Cincinnati Reds—of losing the Series on purpose. Commissioner of Baseball Kenesaw Mountain Landis tossed them out of the game for the rest of their lives.

The players were pitchers Lefty Williams and Eddie Cicotte, shortstop Swede Risberg, outfielders Shoeless Joe Jackson and Happy Felsch, first baseman Chick Gandil, third baseman Buck Weaver, and utility man Fred McMullin. Jackson, Cicotte, and Weaver would probably have been Hall of Famers if it weren't for their involvement.

According to Eliot Asinof, in his book *Eight Men Out*, Risberg got $15,000 from the gamblers who were behind the scheme. Cicotte was paid $10,000. Williams, McMullin, Felsch, and Jackson each got $5,000. Gandil, the ringleader among the players, took $35,000 for his dishonest efforts. This was very big money for all of them. Jackson and Cicotte were making only $6,000 a year. The others made less.

Buck Weaver got nothing. He maintained until the day he died that he should be cleared because he had not participated in throwing ballgames. But he had been present when the other players had discussed what they planned to do, and Judge Landis thought that was just as bad. Weaver was never reinstated.

Most people don't know that the Black Sox were found not guilty in court on a series of five conspiracy counts related to the scandal. The problem was that throwing a baseball game (or a World Series) wasn't against the law. So the prosecution accused them of broader, less specific things, like defrauding the public and injuring the business of the American League. The jury didn't buy it. Of course, it didn't help that while both Jackson and Cicotte had signed confessions, when the time came to enter them into evidence, they had disappeared!

When the jury declared them free, the players thought they would be able to go back to playing big league ball. Landis's judgment shocked them. They all played a little semipro ball (Jackson was still playing—and hitting—into his late forties), then they began settling into life without baseball. Jackson owned a dry cleaners, Weaver a drugstore. Felsch opened a tavern. Cicotte became a game warden in Michigan. Williams, McMullin, Risberg, and Gandil all wound up in California. Some of them, like Cicotte, Williams, and Jackson, gave the impression as the years went by that they were ashamed of what they'd done. Risberg and Gandil, two real tough guys, never seemed to be sorry. Weaver always remained angry that he'd been lumped in with the others.

Let's remember the White Sox players who had nothing to do with the fix in 1919. Manager Kid Gleason. Second baseman Eddie Collins and catcher Ray Shalk (who are in the Hall of Fame). Outfielders Nemo Leibold, Shano Collins, and "Honest Eddie" Murphy. Pitchers Dickie Kerr (who won two games in the Series), Roy Wilkinson, "Big Bill" James, Grover Lowdermilk, and Erskine Mayer. These men are often known as the Clean Sox, because they didn't get involved in the scandal.

The Chicago White Sox of 1919; Joe Jackson is in the top row, second from the right, and Eddie Cicotte is third from the left in the front.

⚾ Why are strikeouts known as K's? ⚾

K is the letter you use to note a strikeout if you are scoring the game. I'd always heard that Henry "Father" Chadwick, the first real baseball writer and the man who invented the score book back in the mid-1800s, was to blame. Chadwick supposedly chose to use the K from the word *struck* because S could stand for too many other things—single, stolen base, shortstop, and so forth. Recently, though, Steve Wulf of *Sports Illustrated* gave the credit to another early sportswriter, M. J. Kelly of the *New York Herald*.

By the way, many scorers use a backward K to show that a player struck out looking—without swinging at the last pitch.

Henry Chadwick, the "Father of Baseball," with his trusty scorebook.

⚾ What was the worst ⚾ major league team of all time?

There have been lots of terrible teams over the years. The most fondly remembered is the 1962 New York Mets. That was the Mets' first year of existence, and it's hard for younger fans to imagine that they were a joke, an awful team that would find all kinds of strange and wonderful ways to lose ballgames. They won only 40 games that year, and lost 120, for a winning percentage of .250. But their fans didn't seem to mind a bit. With manager Casey Stengel keeping the press jolly with the double-talk that the reporters called "Stengelese," the horrible Mets became one of the game's most beloved teams. "Marvelous Marv" Throneberry, the error-prone first baseman who typified the club's inept-

ness, was treated as a cult hero. The 1962 Mets may have been one of the game's worst all-time teams, but they carried it off with a lot of laughs.

Sportscaster Joe Garagiola always picks the 1952 Pittsburgh Pirates as baseball's worst team. He was the Bucs's catcher that year, and they lost 112 games while winning only 42 (.273). The Pirates didn't have the excuse of being an expansion franchise. They were just plain bad. The '52 Pirates had two future broadcasters on the team: Garagiola and the great but aging home-run hitter Ralph Kiner, whose experience with awfulness may have helped him when he began covering the Mets ten years later. They also had two players who were to help a somewhat more talented Pittsburgh team win the World Series in 1960: shortstop Dick Groat and pitcher Bob Friend.

I think an even worse team than the '62 Mets or the '52 Pirates were the Philadelphia Athletics of 1916. Playing for tall, gaunt Connie Mack, the A's racked up (racked down?) a pathetic .238 winning percentage, winning 36 and losing 115. This was extraordinary, because just two years before, the A's had been champions of the American League. Three of the four years before that, they'd been World Champions. But after losing the 1914 Series in four straight to the "Miracle" Boston Braves, Mack broke up his club and sold most of his good players. A new league had sprung up—the Federal League—and its owners were approaching the best A's players with high salary offers. Mack always claimed that he sold his players so they wouldn't just be stolen away. The cure might have been worse than the illness. The A's didn't climb out of the cellar until 1922.

I've always thought that when you talk bad teams, you have to consider the Philadelphia Phillies of 1945. They were 46–108, for a .299 winning percentage. I can hear you saying, "That's bad, but it's not as bad as the Mets or the Pirates or the A's." Right. But 1945 was the last year of World War II. Most of the best players were away in the service. Even the World Series that year was a comedy of errors. Put these Phillies on the field in almost any other year and they might have had trouble winning twenty. Slugger Jimmie Foxx was on this team, but he was old, and he retired at the end of the year. One youngster, catcher Andy Seminick, was good enough to stick around even when the veterans got back, and he helped the Phillies—by then called the Whiz Kids—into the 1950 World Series.

The 1916 A's were probably the worst modern team that didn't have a war as

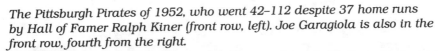

The Pittsburgh Pirates of 1952, who went 42–112 despite 37 home runs by Hall of Famer Ralph Kiner (front row, left). Joe Garagiola is also in the front row, fourth from the right.

an excuse. Taking everything into account, though, I'll go with these 1945 Phillies as the worst team of the twentieth century. But of all time? No way.

Anytime a team finishes the season with more than a hundred losses, it's considered a disaster. Finishing with a winning percentage of under .300—like the '62 Mets, the '52 Pirates, the '45 Phillies, and the '16 A's—indicates truly spectacular ineptitude. But imagine a team finishing up with a winning percentage of under .200! My vote for the worst major league baseball team of all time goes to the 1899 Cleveland Spiders, who won 20 games and lost 134 for the astonishing winning percentage of .130. The previous year, Cleveland had been a respectable 81–68, and the story of how they got so bad so fast is shocking to modern fans.

The club was owned by a man named Frank Robison, who wanted to sell it. The National League, however, had rejected a deal he'd set up. Robison then bought the St. Louis franchise, which gave him control of two teams, a situation that wouldn't be allowed today. Out of spite and to beef up the team in St. Louis, Robison moved most of Cleveland's best players there, including the great pitcher, Cy Young. The result was the 20–134 season.

Dr. Harold Seymour, in his book *Baseball: The Early Years*, says that because they were so bad and had made their fans so angry, the Spiders played most of their games in 1899 in other cities. Smart move!

⚾ Which is the oldest ⚾ ballpark in the big leagues?

Comiskey Park in Chicago, home of the White Sox. It opened in 1910 and was named after the team's owner, Charles Comiskey, who had been a great first baseman for the St. Louis Browns back in the 1880s. The White Sox's ballpark was built to be symmetrical (the same distance down both lines) in an age when that was quite rare. It was also built to be a "pitcher's" park, with very deep fences: 352 feet to the foul poles and 440 feet to dead center field. In 1960, Bill Veeck, who then owned the team, installed baseball's first exploding scoreboard at Comiskey Park. Veeck was famous for experiments and enjoyable oddities. For a while, umpires at Comiskey stocked up on baseballs, not

from the ball boys but from a box on a post that rose up out of the ground.

After Veeck sold the White Sox, the new owners installed synthetic turf on the infield in 1968. When Veeck bought the team back in 1976, he tore up the fake stuff and put real grass down again.

There are three other parks of roughly Comiskey's era still in use in the big leagues. Fenway Park, with its famous left field wall, has been the home of the Boston Red Sox since 1912. Tiger Stadium in Detroit was built in the same year. It was called Navin Field for the first twenty-five years of its existence, after the Tigers' owner, Frank Navin. In 1937, its name was changed to Briggs

Stadium to keep a new owner—Mr. Briggs, of course—happy. It was named Tiger Stadium in 1960. Actually, the Tigers have played on the site of Tiger Stadium since 1901. In those days the field was known as Bennett Park, after Charlie Bennett, a popular old catcher who had lost his legs in an accident. Home plate in Bennett park was in what is now the right field corner, and the old place was completely demolished when Mr. Navin built his new ballpark in 1912.

The third remaining old park is Wrigley Field, which has been the home of the Chicago Cubs since 1916. Actually, Wrigley wasn't built for the Cubs at all but for the rival Chicago Whales of the short-lived Federal League in 1914. Until the 1988 season, Wrigley was the only ballpark in the major leagues without lights. It's still the only one with ivy climbing up its outfield walls.

Many people might say that Yankee Stadium, originally built in 1923, should be part of this list. It would be, but "the House that Ruth built" was torn apart and rebuilt in the mid-1970s. It has totally lost the feel of the grand old Yankee Stadium.

The other famous old big league ballparks have gone: Ebbets Field in Brooklyn, the Polo Grounds in Manhattan, Shibe Park in Philadelphia (and Baker Bowl before it), Crosley Field in Cincinnati (scene of the majors' first

Chicago's Comiskey Park was built in 1910.

night game), Sportsman's Park in St. Louis, Griffith Stadium in Washington D.C., Forbes Field in Pittsburgh. Their strange angles and great character have been replaced by big stadiums that are carpeted with phony grass, are often more suited to football than baseball, and are hard to tell apart. It's too bad.

If you'd like to know more about the big league ballparks, past and present, there are three books you should try to get a look at: *Take Me Out to the Ball Park* by Lowell Reidenbaugh, with drawings by Amadee; *The Ballparks* by Bill Shannon and George Kalinsky, and *Green Cathedrals* by Philip J. Lowry.

⚾ *I know that some teams are expansion* ⚾ *teams and some teams have moved from other cities, but I don't know which are which.*

Keeping track of the teams can be tough. But for a long time, there was no keeping track to do because from 1903 to 1953, no teams moved and not one was added.

It took a while for professional baseball to settle down. During the 1800s, teams moved from city to city and sometimes from league to league. But around the turn of the century, things began to stabilize. The National League dropped four teams from what had been a twelve-team league. The American League came along and made it clear that it was here to stay. From 1903 to 1953, the major leagues were made up of the same sixteen teams, representing the same eleven cities. Nicknames changed from time to time, but basically, the National League looked like this:

The National League:

Boston Braves
Brooklyn Dodgers
New York Giants
Philadelphia Phillies
Pittsburgh Pirates
Cincinnati Reds

Chicago Cubs
St. Louis Cardinals

The American League:

Boston Red Sox
New York Yankees
Philadelphia Athletics
Washington Senators
Cleveland Indians
Chicago White Sox
Detroit Tigers
St. Louis Browns

These cities were all in the northeast quarter of the country—where most of the population lived in 1903. A "western swing" for eastern clubs meant a trip to cities such as Pittsburgh, Cincinnati, Cleveland, Chicago, Detroit, and St. Louis.

The first team to break out of this ancient mold was the Boston Braves, who moved to Milwaukee in 1953. The Braves' move seemed to open the floodgates. The next year, the St. Louis Browns picked up and headed for Baltimore, where they became the Orioles in 1954. The Philadelphia Athletics were

26

next. They jumped to Kansas City in 1955. All these teams had been losing money in their original cities, and their shifts seemed to make good economic sense. Besides, they were all bad teams. Few fans squawked loudly.

But the next teams to move caused a real stir. The Brooklyn Dodgers decided to move to Los Angeles for the 1958 season, and Dodger owner Walter O'Malley persuaded Horace Stoneham of the Giants to bring his team out west too—to San Francisco. Not only was baseball moving way out to the West Coast, but two of its most successful and best-loved teams were shaking loose of their old-time fans. It was a shock many New York and Brooklyn fans still haven't gotten over.

But the Dodgers and Giants had shown the way. The rest of the country wanted baseball. Branch Rickey announced the formation of the Continental League to pressure the National and American Leagues to agree to expansion. (Rickey won his point, and the idea for the Continental League was dropped.)

The American League moved first. In 1961, it added two new teams: the Los Angeles Angels and the Washington Senators. But wait. Wasn't there already a team named the Washington Senators? Yes. But in this year, they moved to Minnesota and became the Twins. The Washington Senators of 1961 were an expansion team. Hang on. We're not done with this one yet.

The National League expanded by two teams the next year. In 1962, the senior circuit brought in the New York Mets and the Houston Colt .45's, which didn't become the Astros until they moved into the Astrodome in 1965—the same year the Los Angeles Angels changed their name to the California Angels.

The next move wasn't long in coming. In 1966, the Braves left Milwaukee for no very good reason and shifted south to Atlanta, thereby becoming the first major league team in this century to move twice. But another team wasn't far behind. In 1968, Charles O. Finley moved his Kansas City (once Philadelphia) Athletics to Oakland.

The following year, 1969, the two leagues expanded again. The National League added the Montreal Expos and the San Diego Padres. The American League took on the Kansas City Royals and the Seattle Pilots. The Pilots didn't last long. By the next season, they were in Milwaukee, doing business as the Brewers. Now each league had twelve teams, and they both went to divisional play.

Remember those new Washington Senators? The ones who took the place of the old Washington Senators, who had become the Minnesota Twins? Well, in 1972, they moved to Texas and became the Rangers. Since then, the nation's capital has been without a baseball team.

After a pretty hectic twenty years, things settled down in baseball for a while after 1972. Then, in 1977, the American League expanded again. It put a team—the Mariners—in Seattle to replace the Pilots, and balanced the western team with a new club in Toronto—the Blue Jays.

Since then, there's been lots of talk but no movement. There will be. Cities like Denver, Washington (again!), Phoenix, New Orleans, and Tampa are working hard to bring a big league club to town.

Here's a brief summary of all teams in both leagues:

National League

Boston Braves became Milwaukee Braves (1953) became Atlanta Braves (1966)

Brooklyn Dodgers became Los Angeles Dodgers (1958)

New York Giants became San Francisco Giants (1958)

Philadelphia Phillies

Pittsburgh Pirates

Cincinnati Reds

Chicago Cubs

St. Louis Cardinals

Expansion Teams

New York Mets (1962)

Houston Colt .45's (1962) became the Astros (1965)

Montreal Expos (1969)

San Diego Padres (1969)

American League

Boston Red Sox

New York Yankees

Philadelphia Athletics became Kansas

City Athletics (1955) became Oakland Athletics (1968)

Washington Senators became Minnesota Twins (1961)

Cleveland Indians

Chicago White Sox

Detroit Tigers

St. Louis Browns became Baltimore Orioles (1954)

Expansion Teams

Los Angeles Angels (1961) became California Angels (1965)

Washington Senators (1961) became Texas Rangers (1972)

Seattle Pilots (1969) became Milwaukee Brewers (1970)

Kansas City Royals (1969)

Seattle Mariners (1977)

Toronto Blue Jays (1977)

What's the difference between ⚾ a slider, a curveball, and a ⚾ screwball? Don't they all curve?

Well, yes. All three are breaking balls, but they're all thrown differently, and they don't all break the same way. The curve breaks the most. It's thrown by cocking the arm and wrist, then snapping them—clockwise for a righthanded pitcher, counterclockwise for a lefty. A righthanded pitcher's curve breaks to the pitcher's left. A lefty's to the pitcher's right. If it's thrown straight overhand, it will drop as well as curve. If it's thrown sidearm, it will break flatter.

The slider was once known as the "nickel curve" because it breaks in the same direction as a curve, but it doesn't break as much. It's thrown faster, with

less wrist snap, and it doesn't drop much. It was used only sporadically until the late '40s or early '50s, but such great pitchers as Ed Walsh and Chief Bender, who pitched in the first two decades of the century, threw a pitch that was the same as today's slider. Steve Carlton may have had the best slider ever. Sparky Lyle based his career as a relief pitcher on his mastery of the pitch. The slider is valuable because it looks like a fastball to the hitter, but it has enough of a break to foul up his timing and swing. Ted Williams hated to face the slider.

The screwball was once renowned as

the "fadeaway" when Christy Mathewson was throwing his for the New York Giants in the early years of the century. It's thrown by cocking the arm and wrist in the opposite way from a curve or a slider, and then snapping the wrist so that the palm faces out from the body. Not surprisingly, it breaks in the opposite direction from curves and sliders.

Carl Hubbell, the Hall of Famer who won 253 games for the Giants from 1928 through 1943, was another artist of the screwball. Today, it's Fernando Valenzuela's specialty. The screwball is a much harder pitch to master than the curve, and it's even harder on the arm.

It's an almost cruelly effective pitch, though.

There's a fascinating book on the topic of breaking balls. It's *The Crooked Pitch* by Martin Quigley.

By the way, don't fool around too much with breaking balls until you're well into your teens. And even then, make sure your arm is ready, then try to find a coach who knows what he's talking about. I missed a whole year of ball when I was in my early teens because I hurt my elbow messing around with the curve. Even then, I never really got the hang of it. If the slider is known as the nickel curve, you might call my pitch "the penny curve."

Christy Mathewson was famed for his "fadeaway," or screwball.

⚾ *Is it true that walks once counted as hits?* ⚾

Yes, it is. For most of baseball history, bases on balls have been officially calculated as no time at bat. They simply do not figure into a player's batting average. In 1887, though, walks counted as hits in the official averages of both the National League and the American Association, which was then a major league.

This was also the first year that batters were not allowed to call for a high or low pitch. Perhaps this was considered such a hardship on hitters that they needed walks counted as hits to make up for it. If so, the move was unnecessary. Under the new rule, eleven men hit over .400—Tip O'Neill of the St. Louis Browns had a stratospheric .492 (which scales down to a still remarkable .435 when you toss out the walks). Rule makers repealed the rule the next year.

Actually, 1887 wasn't the only year when a walk was counted as a time at bat. In 1876—the first year of the National League's existence—they were figured as *outs.* If you took your base, you were credited with a time at bat but no hit. Knowing the strike zone wouldn't have done you much good that year!

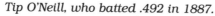

Tip O'Neill, who batted .492 in 1887.

Boy, that's a tough one. My father once saw my uncle make a running bare-handed catch in center field for an amateur team in Waterbury, Connecticut. I know that was a heck of a catch, because people I meet still talk about it fifty years later. That's probably as good a measure as any of a great grab. There's something about a wonderful defensive play that sticks in the minds of spectators longer than anything, except maybe a long, long home run.

In the big leagues, there are a host of catches that have been remembered for years. Here are just a few examples.

Probably the most famous catch of the nineteenth century was made by Bill Lange of Chicago in the mid-1890s. As later sportswriters had it, Lange saved a game against Washington when he chased a Kip Selbach drive deep into center field. Lange supposedly dived full-length for the ball, caught it, began to somersault when he hit the ground, and then smashed right through the outfield fence. A few seconds later, the story goes, he stepped back through the demolished wooden barrier onto the field with the ball in his hand. Selbach was called out, and Chicago won the game.

If this had actually happened, we could stop searching for great catches right now. This would have been it. But researcher Art Ahrens has shown that Lange, a great outfielder who made many fine catches in his career, didn't really crash through the fence. Lange himself only claimed in later years that he had banged into the fence, not that he had gone right through it. Ahrens says that the wonderful—but false—story was the work of Chicago sportswriter Hugh Fullerton, who liked to add even more drama to already impressive events.

Maybe it's because the stakes are so high, but many of the catches fans—and even players—remember best took place in the World Series. The most famous catch of the 1912 Series is one that wasn't made. In the tenth inning of the seventh game, Giant center fielder Fred Snodgrass dropped a routine fly ball. The batter later scored the run that tied the game, which the Red Sox won to take the Series. The "Snodgrass Muff" may be baseball's best-known error. But on the very next play, Snodgrass made what under any other circumstances would have been remembered as one of the great catches in World Series history.

Harry Hooper, the Red Sox's right fielder, hit a long drive into left center. "Ninety-nine times out of a hundred," remembered Hooper years later, "no outfielder could possibly have come close to that ball." But Snodgrass didn't just get close. He ran it down and caught it over his shoulder, robbing Hooper of what everyone in the park thought was a sure triple. Then he whirled, threw to second base, and almost doubled off the runner, who had been running on the play and just barely got back to the base in time. If the Giants had held on to win the Series, people would have been marveling for years about Snodgrass's wonderful defensive abilities. But they lost, and all we hear about is the muff.

In that very same game, Hooper himself made a catch that's been remembered through the years. On a Larry Doyle drive over his head, he raced back, leapt into the air, and caught the ball bare-handed (maybe that's where my uncle got the idea!) before falling over the barrier and into the stands.

Baseball's most controversial catch was made during the 1925 Series between the Washington Senators and the

Pittsburgh Pirates. Pirate Earl Smith hit a long drive to right center field. Senator center fielder Sam Rice ran back, hit the low outfield fence just as he caught the ball, and flipped headfirst into the crowd. He didn't emerge from the stands for a full ten seconds, but when he did, he had the ball in his glove. The umpire called Smith out, and the Pirates hit the roof. They claimed that Rice had spent so much time in the stands because he had lost his grip on the ball and had to wait for Washington fans to retrieve it and get it back to him. For the rest of his life, Rice added fuel to the fire of controversy by refusing to directly answer when he was asked if he'd held on to the ball. "The umpire called him out, didn't he?" Sam would say. But Rice promised that he'd leave a letter telling the whole story to be read after he died. When he passed away in 1974, the letter was read. "At no time," Rice wrote for posterity, "did I lose possession of the ball."

Another great World Series catch was the one the Dodgers' reserve outfielder Al Gionfriddo made off Joe DiMaggio in the sixth game of the 1947 classic. With two men on in the sixth, DiMaggio hit a shot that was long enough to clear the left field bullpen fence over 400 feet from the plate. Gionfriddo, running full-speed toward the bullpen gate, reached over at the last minute and grabbed the ball as it was on its way out. Gionfriddo was a lefthanded fielder, and most observers say that if he'd been a righty, he'd never have been able to stretch his glove across his body to make the catch. DiMaggio was nearly to second base when the catch was made, and there's some great newsreel footage of him kicking the bag in frustration when he realized he'd only get credit for a long out. Although he was a fine fielder, Gionfriddo was a marginal player, and he never made it back to the majors after the 1947 season.

Eight years later, another lefthanded left fielder for the Dodgers, Sandy Amoros, made a great play against the Yankees in the 1955 World Series. And his running catch down the line of a drive by Yogi Berra snuffed out a rally and saved the game—and the Series itself—for Brooklyn.

Twenty years later, the Red Sox's Dwight Evans made an extra-inning catch off the Reds' Joe Morgan that Cincinnati manager Sparky Anderson called one of the two best ever made. Evans got a great start on Morgan's hard liner over his head, caught up to it just in front of the right field stands, and made a leaping, twisting catch, followed by a throw toward first that doubled up runner Ken Griffey.

But how about the other one of

Willie Mays hauls down Vic Wertz's drive in the opening game of the 1954 World Series.

Sparky's "two best catches"? Well, it was another World Series play—one so astonishing that even today it's often still known as "the Catch." In the first game of the 1954 Series between the heavily favored Cleveland Indians and the New York Giants, Vic Wertz of the Indians came up in the ninth inning with the score tied and two men on. Wertz hit a high line drive to deep center that writer Arnold Hano claimed was as hard a shot as he had ever seen in his life. Willie Mays, the Giants' center fielder, turned and ran. And ran. And ran toward the fence, his back to the plate. About 440 feet away from home plate, the ball came down. Mays, slowing slightly so he wouldn't crash into the fence, lifted his hands and caught it over his left shoulder. Then, in a blur of motion, he spun around, his cap flying off, and fired a strike toward second base. It was, says Hano, "the throw of a giant, the throw of a howitzer made human." The Indians failed to score, and the Giants won in ten innings, going on to sweep the Series in four games.

Mays's catch may not have been the greatest catch ever made. In fact, many Mays watchers claim it wasn't even the best catch *Willie* ever made. But the catch off Wertz put together all the elements of great defense in a way that has seldom been seen: speed, judgment, skill, instinct, and pure raw talent. The stuff we go to big league ballgames to see, all wrapped up in a few amazing seconds of whirling movement.

In his book *Fielder's Choice*, Jim Kaplan mentions dozens of great defensive plays. If you're really interested in this topic, check it out.

⚾ What is the highest batting average ⚾ anyone has ever had for one season?

Hold on to your batting helmet! The highest average in baseball history was Tip O'Neil's .492 in 1887. What? *Nobody* can hit .492. Why, only three guys have been within a hundred points of that in the last forty-five years.

You're right. There's a catch. 1887 was the year that walks were counted as hits. Take away his walks, and Tip—an outfielder for the St. Louis Browns—hit a mere .435. And that drops him to second on the all-time list. In 1894, Hugh Duffy of the Boston Beaneaters batted a straight .438, so Duffy holds the all-time single-season record.

Eight men have hit over .400 during the twentieth century. The highest "modern" average is Cardinal Rogers Hornsby's .424 in 1924, one of three times in four years that Rajah went over the magic mark.

Napoleon Lajoie's .422 in 1901 is the highest any American Leaguer has ever hit. But two other American Leaguers, Ty Cobb and George Sisler, hit over .400 twice. Sisler hit .420 in 1922, at a time when he was generally considered to be Cobb's successor as the game's best player. Unfortunately, he began having trouble with his eyes, and his average dropped off over the next few years.

Joe Jackson, Harry Heilmann, Bill Terry, and Ted Williams each batted over .400 once. But poor Joe Jackson didn't even win the batting title when he hit .408 in 1911. That was the year Cobb hit .420. Talk about tough competition!

Williams was the last of the .400 hitters. He came into the last day of the 1941 season just a fraction of a percentage point under the magic mark. If he had sat out that day's doubleheader, his average would have been rounded off to an even .400. His manager offered to let him have the day off so that he could preserve his mark, but he refused. He went 6 for 8 in the two games to raise his average to .406.

Since then, only three hitters have made serious runs at the .400 mark. Williams himself hit .388 in 1957. Rod Carew equaled that mark in 1977. George Brett flirted with .400 all year before settling for .390 in 1980. Somewhere down the line, Wade Boggs or Tony Gwinn or some other great young hitter will probably break the .400 barrier again. But old Hugh Duffy's mark is probably safe for all time.

⚾ What is the prettiest ⚾ ballpark in the big leagues?

Well, I read an article in *Esquire* magazine not long ago that made the flat statement that Dodger Stadium is the most beautiful in baseball. I'm sure there are a lot of people who would agree with that, but there are two or three other parks that would get plenty of votes from fans.

Dodger Stadium is one of the few parks built over the last thirty years that was designed especially for baseball. It's also the first ballpark to welcome more than three million fans through its gates in a single season. It has real grass, it's beautifully maintained, and it's in a lovely setting in the hills. It's a beautiful park, but to me it's only fourth on the list.

Royals Stadium in Kansas City is another modern ballpark that was built just for baseball. I don't like its artificial turf, but I do like the fountains on the embankment beyond the fence in center field. Like Dodger Stadium, Royals Stadium is a great place to watch a ballgame. It's my choice for the third-prettiest baseball stadium.

The other two parks I think are among the prettiest are old-timers. Fenway Park in Boston has been the home of the Red Sox since 1912. During the 1920s and early '30s, it suffered several fires and got really run-down. But then the extremely wealthy Tom Yawkey bought the team. Fenway's been beautifully maintained ever since.

Fenway is the only single-decked stadium in the majors. It's also the strangest-shaped ballpark in the big leagues these days. The right field foul pole is only 302 feet from home plate, and the famous wall in left field—the "Green Monster"—is only 315 feet away down the line. And there are angles everywhere, just waiting to make inexperienced fielders look foolish. Fenway, with its modest green paint, is an old beauty, all right, but my vote for prettiest goes to another old park.

The Cubs have been playing at Wrigley Field in Chicago since 1916. Wrigley has none of the eccentricities of Fenway—unless you count the ivy growing up its brick outfield walls. The park is nearly symmetrical. It has an upper deck. Until 1988 it had no lights. It's

Boston's Fenway Park, with the "Green Monster" in left field.

set in a real neighborhood, with houses and businesses crowded around. I think Wrigley is the model ballpark—a classic that reminds you how things used to be, while continuing to be a great setting for today's game.

⚾ Announcers sometimes tell you how to ⚾ score a certain play, but I'm not sure what the numbers they use mean. Can you help?

This can be a little confusing at first, but once you know the system, it's pretty simple. First off, the numbers used in scoring a ballgame have nothing to do with the numbers on the players' backs, and everything to do with the positions they're playing.

Each position is numbered, starting with the pitcher, then going around the bases, out to the left fielder, and ending with the right fielder. Here we go: pitcher, 1; catcher, 2; first baseman, 3; second baseman, 4; third baseman, 5 (careful here—you have to skip right over the shortstop); shortstop, 6 (got him!); left fielder, 7; center fielder, 8; right fielder, 9. See? Simple. And it's like riding a bike; once you learn the numbers, you never forget them.

There are many ways to score a ballgame—almost everyone I know uses a different method. But every method I've ever seen uses the same basic numbers for players in the field to show what happens to each batter and runner. In almost everybody's system, 6–3, for example, means shortstop (6) to first base (3): the batter grounded to short and was thrown out. F-7 means a fly ball to the left fielder (7). E-5 means an error by the third baseman (5).

Most scorecards you buy at major league parks include a simple set of instructions for scoring a game. But the best way to learn to score is to sit with somebody who's already good at it—the person who scores your local little league or school games, maybe. The wonderful thing about scoring is that you have a record of exactly what happened. It can be great fun years later looking over old score sheets and remembering the great plays and tense situations that you managed to note with simple letters and numbers. Give it a try!

⚾ What was the biggest ⚾ crowd ever to see a ballgame?

Now here's an answer that will surprise you. The best-attended ballgame in history wasn't played in the United States. Or Canada. Or Mexico. Or Cuba. Or Japan. Or any other country you might associate with our national pastime.

No. The ballgame was in Germany. The event was an exhibition night game at the 1936 Olympics. And the crowd was officially reported to the U.S. Olympic Committee as 125,000.

The game was held at the Olympic Stadium in Berlin—the Reichssportfeld. An article on the game by M. E. Travaglini in *The National Pastime* says that there were reports that Nazi dictator Adolf Hitler had demanded that the stands be filled as a matter of national pride. But the Germans crowded to *every* Olympic event that year. Travaglini quotes player Tex Fore as saying, "Yeah, it was a sellout, but they might've had a sellout for an Olympic rooster fight."

The Germans had printed articles about baseball in newspapers, but it was clear the crowd didn't understand the game at all. After putting in an appearance for the opening pitch, thousands left before the game was over.

The next few best-attended game in history also have Olympic connections. Before Dodger Stadium was built, the Dodgers played for a few years in Los Angeles's Memorial Coliseum, which had been built to host the 1932 Olympics and was later used for the 1984 Games as well. On May 7, 1959, the Dodgers met the Yankees in an exhibition game on Roy Campanella Night, which drew a paid crowd of 93,103—the largest baseball crowd in U.S. history. Later that year, crowds almost as big showed up for three games of the World Series between the Dodgers and the Chicago White Sox.

The largest regular-season crowd—84,587—crammed into Cleveland's Municipal Stadium on September 12, 1954, to watch the pennant-bound Indians take on the New York Yankees.

According to Philip J. Lowry, in his book *Green Cathedrals,* the only stadiums that have ever seated more than

70,000 people for a ballgame are the Berlin Reichssportfeld, Memorial Coliseum in Los Angeles, Municipal Stadium in Cleveland, and Yankee Stadium in New York, which used to accommodate over 80,000 fans for really important games. Most newer stadiums today seat 50,000 to 60,000 people, although old Fenway Park in Boston holds only 33,583.

⚾ *What is the smallest crowd* ⚾ *ever to watch a big league game?*

There are a couple of things that hold attendance down. The first is bad weather, usually either very early or very late in the season. The other is a lousy home team that local fans have simply lost interest in. Put the two together and you can get some pretty empty stadiums.

The lowest paid attendance of the twentieth century was 66, at a game in St. Louis's Sportsmen's Park between the Browns and the Detroit Tigers on October 7, 1911. This was the very end of the season, and the Browns had been terrible all year, finishing 45–107. The fans must have been really disgusted, because 1911 was the year Ty Cobb of the Tigers hit .420 and drove in 144 runs on 248 hits. I'd sit through a likely home-team loss to watch him play, wouldn't you?

In more recent times, the terrible Red Sox of 1965 pulled only 409 fans into Fenway Park for a game against the Angels on September 29 of that year. And there were only 38 people in the stands at Shea when the Mets opened a doubleheader against the Phillies on September 16, 1981. In *Green Cathedrals,* though, Phil Bess points out that the official paid attendance was over 4,000.

It's actually a great treat to be in the ballpark when not too many other fans have decided to come out. You miss the excitement of a large crowd, but you can get better seats, and you feel closer to the game because you can *hear* more of what's happening on the field. I remember going to a game at Fenway Park at the tail end of the Red Sox's disappointing 1976 season. There were only a few thousand people in the park, and I was able to grab a seat right behind the visitors' dugout. From there, and because the place was so quiet, I could hear coaches talking to players, retired batters complaining to on-deck men, the shortstop snapping instructions to the second baseman. Low attendance is bad for the teams' pocketbooks, but it can be great fun if you're one of the few to show up.

Quick, now. Have you ever heard of the Union Association? How about the Players' League? Well, these were two of the seven major leagues baseball has seen over the last hundred and twenty years or so.

There's an argument over which was the first major league. Most historians would probably tell you that it was the National Association of Professional Base Ball Players. I think they're right, but the Special Baseball Records Committee, sanctioned by organized baseball, disagrees. It doesn't count the NA among big leagues, "due to its erratic schedule and procedures."

The Committee has a point. The National Association, which was founded in 1871 and lasted only five years, wasn't very well organized. Teams arranged their own schedules. The only requirement was that a team play each other team in the Association five times in a season. In 1874, Boston and Philadelphia disrupted the season by heading off for an exhibition tour of England, where they also played cricket. But the game's best players and best teams played in the NA. I think it deserves to be considered major.

In 1876, the National League was founded in an attempt to put professional baseball on a sounder business footing. Where the National Association was a grouping of *players*, the National League was a grouping of *clubs*. Schedules were made up by a central office. Teams were forced to do things the league's way. No more mid-season exhibition tours.

The National League had a tough few years getting going, but by the early 1880s, it was doing well enough to attract competition. The American Association was established in 1881, and started play in 1882. Its teams played ball on Sundays, set ticket prices at 25 cents—half the National League's charge—and many teams in the Association sold alcohol at their parks. The "beer and whiskey" Association did quite well during much of the 1880s. It had many great players, such as the great first baseman Charlie Comiskey, and several great teams. Comiskey's St. Louis Browns may have been the best club of the era in any league. Toward the end of the 1880s, though, the Association's leadership weakened, and the AA eventually died in 1891.

The Union Association is probably the least-known of the major leagues. It was promoted by a man named Henry V. Lucas, partly because he wanted a team in the National League and couldn't get one. The National League and the American Association fought hard against it, and the Union Association lasted only a single year: 1884.

The Players' League of 1890 may have been the most interesting major league, but it also lasted only one year. It was established when many professional ballplayers, including most of the game's great names, got fed up with the way the National League and the American Association were using the reserve clause to keep salaries down. Dozens and dozens of players simply quit their teams in the other circuits and formed their own league. Led by the remarkable player and lawyer John Montgomery Ward, many of the players invested their own money in their clubs. By most accounts, the Players' League drew more fans in 1890 than either the NL or the AA. All three leagues lost money, but the PL's wealthy backers were tricked into thinking that the National League was in strong financial shape, and they gave up, selling out to National League owners in most cases.

The NL immediately reimposed the reserve clause, drove the weakened AA out of business, reduced salaries, and established a big league monopoly that lasted right through the 1890s.

That monopoly was finally broken by the American League, which had started as the Western League during the 1890s. Its president, Ban Johnson, wanted to make it a major league, so he renamed it, gathered solid baseball men like Connie Mack and Charles Comiskey as owners, and moved teams into bigger cities at the turn of the century. By 1901, Johnson and his American League were fighting the National League tooth and nail for players and fan support. The National League soon realized that it had met its match, and it signed the National Agreement, setting up the basic structure under which big league baseball still operates.

There was one more league war to fight, though. In 1914 and 1915, the Federal League went head to head against the established structure. The owners of Federal League clubs paid a number of established stars a lot of

Ban Johnson, who founded the American League.

money to join their teams, and many of them did. The Federal League collapsed, though, when it lost an important lawsuit that charged the American and National Leagues of being illegal monopolies.

Since 1915, there have been rumblings of new major leagues, but there has been no serious threat to the position of the National and American Leagues at the top of the baseball world.

⚾ Why don't all teams put their players' ⚾ names on the backs of their uniforms?

Well, baseball's a very traditional game, and some teams just don't want to. Unlike the National Football League, baseball has no rule making names on uniforms mandatory.

The first baseball team to put players' names on their jerseys was the Chicago White Sox in 1960. It was, like so many other new things, the idea of Bill Veeck, who owned the Sox at the time. Up until then, spectators had to be content with memorizing their favorite players' numbers.

Numbers themselves didn't appear on baseball players' backs until the Cleveland Indians started wearing them in 1916. They *are* mandatory, and have been since the early 1930s. When the great Yankee team of the '20s adopted jersey numbers, they were assigned to starters according to the player's place in the batting order. That's why Babe Ruth wore his famous number 3, and cleanup hitter Lou Gehrig buttoned on jersey number 4.

What was the greatest team in baseball history?

The team that won the most games during a regular season was the 1906 Chicago Cubs. They won 116 while losing only 36, and then won the National League pennant by a full twenty games over a very good New York Giants team. This was the Cub squad with the famous double-play combination of Tinker, Evers, and Chance, and the great pitcher Mordecai "Three Finger" Brown.

The Cubs swept into the World Series that year as heavy favorites over their crosstown rivals, the White Sox. The Sox were nicknamed "the Hitless Wonders" because they'd won the American League pennant despite the lowest team batting average in the league. But they surprised almost everyone and knocked off the Cubs in six games. Those Cubs were great, all right, but if we're looking for the greatest team of all time, I don't think we can choose one that lost the World Series, do you?

That lets out the 1954 Cleveland Indians too. That year the Indians set the all-time American League record for games won during the regular season: 111. They had to be great that year, because the New York Yankees won 103 games, normally more than enough to secure the pennant. The Indians were a powerful offensive team that also had baseball's best pitching, featuring a "big four" of Early Wynn, Bob Lemon, Mike Garcia, and Bob Feller. But they lost the World Series in four straight games to the New York Giants.

This doesn't *always* happen, of course. Many teams have pounded their opposition all season and then gone on to win the series too. The 1909 Pittsburgh Pirates, featuring the great Honus Wagner, won 110 regular-season games to take the National League pennant, then went on to beat Ty Cobb's Tigers four games to three in the Series.

Similarly, the 1961 Yankees were 109–53 during the regular season, while Mickey Mantle hit 54 homers and Roger Maris broke Babe Ruth's mark with 61. In the Series, they battered the Cincinnati Reds four games to one behind the superb pitching of Whitey Ford, who won two games and allowed no runs at all.

But let's look at the two teams that most often are compared when the topic of the greatest team comes up: the 1927 Yankees and the 1976 Cincinnati Reds.

The 1927 Yankees was the team of Babe Ruth and Lou Gehrig. In 1927, the Babe hit his 60 homers, and Lou drove in 175 runs. They blasted through the American League, winning 110 of 154 games. Then they swept the Pirates four straight in the World Series.

Cincinnati's Big Red Machine of 1976 was also a potent offensive force, with men like Tony Perez, Joe Morgan, Johnny Bench, George Foster, and Pete Rose in the lineup. They won 102 games in the regular season, then swept the Philadelphia Phillies (who themselves had gone 101–61) in the League Championship Series before whitewashing the Yankees 4–0 in the World Series.

The remarkable thing about these two teams is that they had on their rosters four men who are arguably the all-time All-Stars at their positions: Johnny Bench behind the plate, Lou Gehrig at first base, Joe Morgan at second, and Babe Ruth in the outfield.

Comparisons are awfully hard to make, because the teams played in different eras. Overall, though, the Reds

The 1927 New York Yankees, featuring Lou Gehrig (top row, left) and Babe Ruth (top, third from left).

were probably a bit better than the Yankees defensively, especially "up the middle." Pat Collins and Johnny Grabowski can't compare with Bench at catcher. New York's Mark Koenig was considered a fine shortstop, but the Reds' Dave Concepcion was faster and had more range. At second base the Yankees' Tony Lazzeri was no slouch, but he's up against one of the very best in Morgan. In center, Cesar Geronimo had more speed and range than New York's excellent Earle Combs.

Offensively, both teams were absolutely explosive. The Yankee lineup came to be known as "Murderers' Row," and sportswriters talked about "five-o'clock lightning" because the Yanks always seemed to bust loose and bury their opponents late in games. Cincinnati manager Sparky Anderson called the hitters on his team "my big coconuts," and he always knew that the Big Red Machine was never really out of a game.

Yankee pitching was better, with arms like Waite Hoyt, Herb Pennock, and Urban Shocker. In 1927, the Yanks also had one of baseball's early relief specialists in Wilcy Moore. For the Reds, Anderson won the nickname Captain Hook because he had to go to the bullpen so often. The result was that reliever Rawley Eastwick led the National League with 26 saves.

So where does that leave us? If it weren't for the pitching, I'd lean toward the Reds, but I think I'll stick with the classic pick—the 1927 New York Yankees. It's so close, though, that you could look at the same set of players and statistics and come to the other conclusion.

Wouldn't it be great if we could get these guys together in some baseball heaven and let 'em play a sort of all-time World Series?

⚾ I heard a broadcaster talk about a ⚾ "phantom" double play. What is that?

A "phantom" double play is one where the infielder who is supposed to touch second base to force out the lead runner doesn't do so, but the umpire calls the runner out, anyway. This happens a lot. Why?

Double plays usually start with the shortstop fielding a grounder and tossing the ball to the second baseman to force the runner at second. The second baseman then relays the ball to the first baseman to get the batter.

When the second baseman catches the shortstop's throw, he has to perform what's called his "pivot." He receives the ball while he's looking—and sometimes moving—toward the shortstop, and then he must very quickly turn and fire the ball to first.

As he begins his pivot, the second baseman is in about the most dangerous position there is in baseball. While he's looking one way, trying to catch a ball and tag a base, there's a runner barreling in from behind him who wants to hit him hard enough to keep him from throwing—or at least throwing accurately—to first. In the last decade or so, runners have more and more gone in for the so-called "rolling block" when they come in to second base. They start a slide but don't stay down, really trying to reach the base. Instead, they keep their upper bodies well off the ground and try to twist and roll right into the pivot man. They often go right outside the baseline to knock down the second baseman, even if he's not yet making his play at the base.

Not surprisingly, second basemen often try to stay out of danger by relaying the ball to first without actually touching second base. This makes it easier for them to stay out of the way of the incoming runner. Especially if the play doesn't look very close, umpires will almost always call the runner out.

Real old-timers will tell you that this sort of thing didn't happen years ago, and that runners coming into second base were not allowed to go after the pivot man away from the base, or to execute the rolling block. On the other hand, fans and sportswriters have been complaining about the phantom double play for at least forty years.

There have also been second basemen who weren't fazed by the assaults of baserunners. Little Nellie Fox, the White Sox second baseman who was the American League's Most Valuable Player in 1959, was famous for getting knocked over all the time on his pivot, but he claimed that he always scrambled to his feet before the runner could get up. And the Pirates' husky Bill Mazeroski was known as Tree Stump because he was that solid when he had his foot on the base during a pivot. Runners colliding with him felt as if they'd run into a stump too. One was shaken up so badly that he had to be carried off the field on a stretcher.

Umpires could probably stop the phantom double play if they did two things. First, they could call interference on any runner who did more than slide aggressively into second. Then they could force the pivot man to actually touch the base on a double play.

This will probably never happen. Most players and managers are content with things the way they are, and there would be a huge uproar if umpires suddenly began enforcing the rule against interference. That's too bad, because a real double play executed under fair pressure from a sliding runner is one of baseball's great beauties. But you'll still be seeing the phantom double play when you're as old as I am.

⚾ *What is the "hot stove league"?* ⚾

I've always thought that this old phrase conjured up one of the game's most pleasant images. Just imagine a small group of baseball fans in winter. They live in a small town somewhere—as most people did eighty or a hundred years ago—and in the winter they like to gather at the general store, where they sit around the old potbellied stove, nibble on soda crackers, play checkers, and gossip about whatever comes to mind.

Naturally, what usually comes to mind is baseball. But since it's the off-season, they can't talk about how Walter Johnson is pitching, or how well Brooklyn's doing, or what McGraw's doing with the Giants. Instead, they reminisce, going back over the season that recently ended, talking "what-ifs" and "shoulda beens." And they wonder about trades that might be coming up, and what their favorite teams' chances are come April.

Cozy baseball gossip in the off-season, that's what the hot stove league is. One of the game's best traditions—even though these days it usually takes place around a water fountain at work or over a school desk.

⚾ *How many unassisted triple plays* ⚾ *have there been in the big leagues?*

This is one of baseball's rarest sights. Only eight men in major league history have turned the trick. Oddly, six of them accomplished their feats during the 1920s. Two were performed within a month's time in 1923. And two more came on successive days in 1927.

The most famous unassisted triple play is the one turned in by the Cleveland Indians' second baseman Bill Wambsganss during the 1920 World Series against the Brooklyn Dodgers. With men on first and second, Wamby ran to his right to make a nice catch of pitcher Clarence Mitchell's line drive. He kept going to step on second before Pete Kilduff could return to the base, then turned around and ran over to tag Otto Miller, who had gotten so confused that he had stopped in the baseline on his way to second. Wamby's historic play didn't get as much space in the papers the next day as you might expect, because the reporters of the day were

Second from the left is Cleveland shortstop Neal Ball, who made the major leagues' first unassisted triple play. With him are the three Red Sox he put out (from the left), Amby McConnell, Heinie Wagner, and Jake Stahl.

a lot more excited by teammate Elmer Smith's grand-slam home run—the first in Series history.

The first regular-season unassisted triple play took place in 1909, and it was a Cleveland infielder's effort that time too. This time it was a shortstop, Neal Ball, but the action was essentially the same. Ball caught a Red Sox line drive, stepped on second, and tagged the man coming from first.

In 1923, first baseman George Burns of the Boston Red Sox really had to work for his triple play. He caught a drive off the bat of Cleveland's Frank Brower (Cleveland again? Yup.), stepped on first, and then sprinted for second base, where he slid in just ahead of the runner who had broken for third and was trying to get back.

Just a few weeks later, the National League got its first unassisted triple play. The Boston Braves' rookie shortstop, Ernie Padgett, made it against the Phillies in the standard way. He caught a line drive, stepped on second, and tagged the man coming from first.

Shortstop Glenn Wright of the Pirates was next. In early 1925, he took a drive off the bat of the Cardinals' Sunny Jim Bottomley, touched second to double off Cardinal shortstop Jim Cooney, then tagged Rogers Hornsby coming from first.

That same Jim Cooney wrote himself into the record books two years later. On May 30, 1927, now playing short for the Chicago Cubs, he caught a liner hit by the Pirate's Paul "Big Poison" Waner, touched second to force Lloyd "Little Poison" Waner, and then tagged Clyde Barnhart, who was running from first. Cooney became the first—and so far the only—person to be involved in two unassisted triple plays: once as victim and once as perpetrator.

The very next day, May 31, 1927, first baseman Johnny Neun of the Detroit Tigers caught a line drive, stepped on first to double the runner there, and

44

then ran across the diamond to tag Glenn Myatt, who had gone almost all the way to third.

After Neun's effort, it was over forty years before baseball saw another unassisted triple play. Washington Senators shortstop Ron Hansen turned the trick in 1968. I bet you know how he did it. Right: catch line drive, touch second, tag man from first.

I sure would like to see one of these someday, wouldn't you?

⚾ *I've read that a player* ⚾ *once tripled into a triple play. Is this true? How could it happen?*

The player in question was Floyd Caves "Babe" Herman, who played for Brooklyn in the late '20s and early '30s when they were known more for their clownish ineptitude than for their ability to play ball. The press called them "the Daffiness Boys" and the daffy boy they often had in mind was Babe Herman.

Herman was a fine hitter who compiled a lifetime average of .324, but he's best-known for his adventures in right field and on the basepaths. Actually, though, Herman didn't triple into a triple play. He doubled into a double play, which is hard enough. Here's what happened.

It was August 1926. In the bottom of the seventh at Ebbet's Field in a game against the Boston Braves, rookie Herman came to the plate with the score tied 1–1 and the bases loaded. Catcher Hank DeBerry was on third, pitcher Dazzy Vance occupied second, and second baseman Chick Fewster was over at first. Herman promptly hit a line drive to right field, which would normally have scored at least two runs, maybe three. He rounded first, dug for second, and slid in easily with a double.

But as he began to get up, Babe noticed a Brooklyn player in a rundown between third and home. He figured it was Fewster, the man who'd been on first. In this situation, baserunners are trained to move up and take the base behind the rundown. So Herman headed for third. But when he got there, he was in for a surprise. Fewster was already on the base, standing there watching the rundown in progress down the line.

Just then, the trapped Brooklyn runner escaped from the rundown and slid into third from the home-plate side. It

Babe Herman, who did not triple into a triple play—but came mighty close.

turned out to be Vance, a tortoiselike runner who had gotten a very slow start on Herman's hit and had been unable to score from second.

The Boston third baseman didn't waste time trying to figure out the rules; he just tagged every Brooklyn uniform within reach. Fewster and Herman were quite properly called out by the umpire because the base belonged to Vance.

The upshot was that Babe got credit for a double, so he had doubled into a double play even though the action took place at third. It's probably the most famous silly play in baseball history, and it perfectly represents the Dodgers of that era, but people forget one important thing: Babe's hit scored DeBerry with what turned out to be the game's winning run.

⚾ Who is the best pitcher in baseball history? ⚾

Well, I'm going to get into trouble no matter what I say here, so let me start this way: My personal all-time favorite pitcher is Warren Spahn. "Spahnnie" was the picture of what sportswriters mean when they talk about "classy southpaws." Pitching mostly for the Braves, he won 363 games from 1942 through 1965—the most of any left-hander in history. He has a legitimate claim to be one of the all-time greats. And he had something extra that made him special: elegance. He used the kind of big, smooth, almost double-pumping windup that has disappeared from the game today, and he threw with a beautiful, fluid, pure overhand motion. Warren Spahn *looked* more like a pitcher than any other pitcher I ever saw.

Four other hurlers—all righthanders —won more games than Spahn during their careers: Cy Young, Walter Johnson, Christy Mathewson, and Grover Cleveland Alexander.

Cy Young won the incredible total of 511 to top the list. Young also *lost* more games than any pitcher in history: 313. Cy still holds records for complete games and innings pitched. He was a great pitcher for a long time. It's said that he was still throwing well when he retired during spring training in 1912

but that he'd gained so much weight, he couldn't bend over fast enough to field bunts.

Walter Johnson is the only other pitcher to have won more than 400 games. Every one of his 416 wins from 1907 to 1927, was for a Washington Senator club that was usually pretty bad. Until Steve Carlton, Nolan Ryan, and Gaylord Perry broke it, the Big Train held the record for most career strikeouts. Johnson, who threw with a whiplike sidearm motion, was a pure fastball pitcher, often called the fastest who ever threw a baseball. Ty Cobb and many others called him baseball's greatest pitcher, and some students of the game have run mathematical studies that agree.

Christy Mathewson gets many of the votes Johnson doesn't. Matty pitched for John McGraw's New York Giants from 1900 to 1916, winning 373 games in the process. Like Johnson, he was an admirable character, as well as being one of his league's best pitchers year after year. Mathewson's most famous pitch was his "fadeaway," which we would call a screwball. He also had a very effective curve and, early in his career, a good fastball. He pitched for one of baseball's best teams and was

46

involved in many of the most dramatic events of his era. He is one of the game's great legendary personalities.

Grover Cleveland Alexander was known as Pete. He pitched in the National League for Philadelphia, Chicago, and St. Louis from 1911 to 1930, and he picked up where Mathewson left off as the league's best hurler. His best pitch is sometimes described as a sinking fastball, but it was really more like a hard screwball because it moved in sharply on righthanded batters. The pitch created a callus on Alexander's finger, and every year in spring training he had to build that callus back up, a painful process that started out with a blister. Each season his teammates waited for Pete's callus to develop, and when he started getting batters out regularly, they knew his finger had toughened up and he was ready for the season.

Aside from these five top winners, there are other pitchers who have to be considered among the best of all time. Lefty Grove won 300 games, even though he didn't get to the majors un-til he was 25 years old. In his *Historical Abstract*, Bill James makes the flat statement that Grove was the best of all, and explains why he thinks so: He led his league in Earned Run Average nine times (to Mathewson's, Johnson's, and Alexander's five), and he led in winning percentage five times—more than anyone else ever has. Grove pitched for the great Athletics champions of 1929–1931, and he was equally well known for his blazing fastball and his fiery temper.

Dizzy Dean of the Cardinals was almost unbeatable for a few years during the early '30s, but his career was cut short by injury, and we'll never know how good he could have been over a long career. With the Cardinals, he once pitched a three-hitter in the first game of a doubleheader against Brooklyn, only to see his brother Paul (also known as Daffy) toss a no-hitter in the second game. "Paul didn't tell me he was gonna throw a no-hitter," Diz is reported to have said. I'da known that, I'da throwed one too."

Walter Johnson was known as the "Big Train" because of his awesome fastball.

Bob Feller won 266 games for the Indians, even though he, like so many players, lost more than three years to the service during World War II. He won 25 games the year before he left, and 26 the year after got back, so its probably safe to assume he would have won well over 300 if his career hadn't been interrupted.

Sandy Koufax was about as dominant as a pitcher can be for four years during the 1960s, but he'd pitched in the big leagues for eight years before he exploded into greatness, and he retired from baseball when he was only 30.

More recently, Tom Seaver and Steve Carlton have put together long careers that compare with the greatest ever.

There have been so many great ones that it's almost impossible to pick the single top pitcher. How about picking a staff? That's tough, too, but let's give it a try. Righthanders: Johnson and Mathewson. Lefthanders: Spahn and Grove. And with all the superb pitchers left over, just imagine the bullpen!

✎ Why doesn't the National ✎ League use the designated hitter?

Nobody used the designated hitter until 1973. It was adopted by the American League that year in an attempt to add some offensive punch. The National League, which had been clearly superior for a number of years and didn't feel it needed any help to score runs, scorned this revolutionary change to the rules of the game.

Other leagues, from the minors all the way down to school leagues, Little League, and even softball leagues, latched on the idea of the designated hitter, many of them because it let them get more players into the game—not a bad reason in kids' leagues.

The National League is now just about the only organization in the baseball world in which the pitcher hits.

Ever since the DH was introduced on the major league level, there's been a lot of debate over it. I once heard former Commissioner Bowie Kuhn say that it was simple: American League fans liked the rule and National League fans didn't. I think Kuhn was wrong. It seems to me that most younger fans like the DH, or at least accept it as normal, while most older fans, who grew up without the rule, don't.

Old fogy that I am, I don't like it myself. The idea of having a guy on the team who doesn't have to play the whole game bothers me. In years past, a good hitter who was a lousy fielder might never make it in the big leagues because his poor defense would hurt the team too much. Now, in the American League, that guy can become a star. He doesn't have to be a ballplayer, just a hitter. In theory, a guy could come along and break Henry Aaron's home-run record without ever playing an inning in the field. That seems out of whack to me.

Will the National League ever accept the DH? Not anytime soon, that's for sure. The NL still makes it clear that it is proud not to have stooped to accepting what it calls a "gimmick." Will the American League ever dump the DH? That's not likely, either. It's been in place for over fifteen years, it's become part of the AL game, and all those youngsters coming up are used to it.

The All-Star Game as we know it got started in Chicago in 1933. The Windy City was holding its Century of Progress Exposition that year, and a man named Arch Ward, who was the sports editor of the Chicago *Tribune*, thought a game between each league's best players would be a great addition to the celebration. Ward's game was supposed to be a onetime affair, but Babe Ruth christened the event with a home run, and the response from fans to the game was so great that it quickly became an annual celebration.

Except for the war year of 1945, an All-Star Game has been held every season since. (Actually, from 1959 through 1962, there were *two* All-Star Games each year.) The Game has seen some marvelous performances. In 1934, Giant screwballer Carl Hubbell struck out, in order, Babe Ruth, Lou Gehrig, Jimmy Foxx, Al Simmons, and Joe Cronin, as tough a murderers' row as any pitcher's ever had to face. In 1941, Ted Williams hit a three-run homer with two outs in the bottom of the ninth to win the game for the American League. Five years later

Babe Ruth hits home plate after bashing a home run in the 1933 All-Star Game.

he hit one out on Rip Sewell's famous "eephus" pitch, a ball that Sewell tossed softly to the plate in a high arc. In 1950, Red Schoendeinst of the Cardinals hit a fourteenth-inning home run to win one for the National League. During the '60s, Willie Mays seemed to run wild every year as the National League began to dominate in All-Star play. In 1971, the young Reggie Jackson hit a memorably titanic shot off a right field light stanchion in Detroit.

Actually, Ward's game wasn't the first to gather great stars for an exhibition. Way back in 1858, a squad of New York's best players had gathered from several teams and played the All-Stars of Brooklyn. And in 1887, Albert Spalding had taken his Chicago White Stockings and a picked team he called the All-Americas on a world tour. The two teams played each other across the United States, on to Hawaii and the South Seas, into Australia, across the Indian Ocean, up the Red Sea to Egypt, and through Italy, France, and England before returning home and playing their way from New York back to Chicago.

In later years, players would often get together to barnstorm (and make a little extra money) after the season was over. In this way, the best white and black players often got to test each other's skills in the days when major league baseball was for whites only.

Perhaps the best-known early All-Star Game was the one held in 1911 to raise money for the widow of the great Cleveland pitcher, Addie Joss, who had died of meningitis at the age of 31. The players assembled to play against the Indians included Ty Cobb, Tris Speaker, Eddie Collins, Home Run Baker, Sam Crawford, Walter Johnson, and Bobby Wallace—Hall of Famers all. There's a famous photo of this squad, assembled in front of the stands before the game. In it, Tiger star Cobb is wearing a Cleveland uniform. The story is that he had a heavy cold and had decided not to play, but that he changed his mind when he arrived at the park and had to borrow a suit to play in. Imagine looking at a photo and seeing Wade Boggs sitting there in a Twins uniform. Or Dale Murphy dressed as a Dodger. It sure would make you take a second look, wouldn't it?

⚾ *Who had the fastest fastball of all time?* ⚾

Oh, my. There's really no way to answer this question for sure. Years ago, they had no way to measure accurately the speed of a pitch, and even today, different radar guns register different speeds.

Nolan Ryan's heater has been timed at over 100 miles an hour. Bob Feller, the great Indian fastballer of the late '30s, '40s, and early '50s, was timed once at over 98 miles an hour, but the test required him to fire the ball into a sort of box, and before everything worked properly, his fastest pitches of the day were behind him.

As you probably know from listening to sportscasters on televised games, anything over 90 miles an hour is pretty fast. Pitches in the mid-90s are *really* fast.

There's something extra nasty about great fastballs, though. They "move." Because of the very fast backward rotation on a hard fastball, the ball will often rise as it nears the plate. At 90-something miles an hour, this happens very fast—you sometimes hear broadcasters saying that a pitch like this "exploded"—and it's almost impossible for a batter to handle. Other, usually less speedy fastballs can be thrown so they move in or out a little, or even sink a bit.

There are many names in the fastballing hall of fame. During the 1890s, Amos Rusie was known as the Hoosier Thunderbolt, and it's said that he is responsible for the pitching distance being moved back to its current sixty feet, six inches.

Walter Johnson is still the name people think of first when fast pitching comes up. Nick Altrock, who was an American League pitcher in the early part of the century when Johnson was active, once said that if there had been night ball when the Big Train was pitching, Congress would have passed a law against him. His whole career, Johnson threw only the fastball. He never bothered with a curve.

In his own era, Johnson was challenged as speed king for a short time by Smokey Joe Wood. Wood's pitching career was cut short by injuries, but Johnson himself said, "Can I throw harder than Joe Wood? Listen, my friend, there's no man alive can throw harder than Smokey Joe Wood."

Since Johnson and Wood, big league

Top, right: Nolan Ryan, whose fastball has been clocked at over 100 miles per hour. Left: Smokey Joe Wood's fastball propelled him to record of 34–5 in 1912, plus three more wins in the World Series. Bottom, right: Bob Feller, here with Joe DiMaggio, was the fastest pitcher of his day, and perhaps all time.

baseball has seen such smoke-throwers as Lefty Grove, Dazzy Vance, Dizzy Dean, Feller, and Sandy Koufax, right on to Tom Seaver, Goose Gossage, Nolan Ryan, and Roger Clemens.

Some of these guys—Clemens is a good example today—had pinpoint control; some, like Koufax, were wild men who finally learned to put the ball where they wanted it. Other fireballers never really made it big because they never had an idea of where their bullets would go. There was a minor leaguer in the Baltimore chain named Steve Dalkowski whom many people thought might be the hardest thrower ever. He never mastered his control, though, and didn't make it to the majors. And somebody once said of the Dodgers' Rex Barney, for example, that he could throw a baseball through a brick wall—if he could hit the wall.

Who was fastest? Who knows. Just be glad you don't have to hit against any of them—yet, anyway.

Who invented the curveball?

You might not know this, but there used to be a real dispute over whether curveballs actually curved. Many people (obviously not the type who had ever actually tried to hit a breaking ball) maintained that the curve was simply an optical illusion. Many demonstrations were set up to convince these skeptics, during which pitchers would bend throws around stakes driven into the ground.

The man who usually gets credit for inventing the curve is Arthur "Candy" Cummings, who began throwing one during club games in the mid-1860s. The rules at the time forced pitchers to toss the ball underhand, so Candy's curve probably broke only to the side, not to the side and down, like those thrown by the overhand pitchers of today. Cummings had a fine, if short, career in professional baseball.

Another pitcher sometimes called the first curveballer is Bobby Mathews, who worked for a Maryland club called the Lord Baltimores at about the same time as Cummings was pitching for clubs in the New York area. Evidence suggests, though, that the breaking ball thrown by Mathews was more likely a spitter than a true curve.

There are also suggestions that the

A young Candy Cummings, here pictured on the right, is thought to have originated the curveball.

52

first curves thrown in games were snapped off by pitchers at Eastern prep schools and colleges, and that they made their way into semiprofessional and professional baseball later.

Candy Cummings, though, is the man who is recognized by baseball itself as the inventor of the curve. And he has a plaque on the wall of the Hall of Fame to prove it!

⚾ Has anyone ever really "killed the ump"? ⚾

In the old days, umpires took even more grief than they do today. There are many stories of umps having to be escorted from ballparks after games by the police, and even of players protecting them from angry fans by swinging bats.

Umpires in the big leagues have been bumped, kicked, spat on, and punched. A husky fan once ran out on the field and attacked George Magerkirth. Ty Cobb and umpire Bill Evans once met to mix it up under the stands. But no big league ump has ever died in the line of duty. Unfortunately, the same cannot be said of the minor leagues.

In 1899, Sam White was umpiring a game at Loundesborough, Alabama. Players had been arguing with his calls all day. Finally, when a player actually threatened him, White punched him. The player got up and hit White over the head with a bat, killing him.

Two years later, in Farmersburg, Indiana, Umpire Ora Jennings was also killed when a player struck him with a bat.

⚾ Is it true that two opposing pitchers ⚾ once pitched no-hitters in the same game?

Sort of. On May 2, 1917, Hippo Vaughn of the Chicago Cubs and Fred Toney of the Cincinnati Reds went at each other in Wrigley Field. Neither allowed a hit through nine innings, but Vaughn lost his no-hitter and his shutout in the top of the tenth. Toney shut the Cubs down in the bottom half of the inning. So while both men pitched nine innings of no-hit ball, and received credit for no-hitters, only Toney showed a win for his effort. Vaughn lost one of the great heartbreakers of all time.

An even tougher loss was suffered by Harvey Haddix of the Pittsburgh Pirates. On a cool night in May 1959, Haddix started a game against the defending National League champion Braves in Milwaukee's County Stadium. Using a live fastball and a sharply breaking slider, Haddix mowed down the hard-hitting Braves inning after inning. Through nine innings, no Brave had gotten a hit or a walk. No Brave had reached base at all. Haddix was pitching a perfect game. But his opposite number, Lew Burdette had been tough too. He'd allowed the Pirates five hits but no runs. So Haddix had to keep going. He set down the Braves in the tenth, the eleventh, and the twelfth, but Burdette was keeping pace, and the Pirates couldn't score.

Finally, in the bottom of the thirteenth, the Braves got their first baserunner of the game when Pirate third baseman Don Hoak made a wild throw to first on a ground ball hit to him by Felix Mantilla. Everything unraveled from there. Eddie Mathews sacrificed Mantilla to second. Haddix walked Hank Aaron intentionally to set up the double play, and then Joe Adcock belted a high slider out of the park—the Braves' only hit of the game. In the space of a few minutes, Haddix lost a perfect game, a no-hitter, a shutout, and a ballgame. And all after twelve innings of the most amazing pitching performance anyone's ever seen.

Jim "Hippo" Vaughn (below) threw a no-hitter through nine innings—and lost, as his opponent, Fred Toney (above), threw a no-hitter for ten frames.

⚾ What's the longest winning ⚾ streak any team has ever had?

The 1916 New York Giants won an amazing 26 in a row. Earlier in the same season, they had won 17 straight. But the most incredible thing about their season was that despite these two long winning streaks, they finished not first but fourth!

How did such a strong team fail to win the pennant going away? Fred Lieb, a well-known sportswriter who covered the club in those days, said that the streaks were a result of playing the four weakest clubs in the league all in a row. In 1916, the weak teams in the National League happened to be the ones out west: St. Louis, Pittsburgh, Chicago, and Cincinnati. The schedule was set up so that all of the teams from the east or west (there were no formal divisions at the time) would be touring the other part of the country at the same time.

Early in the season, the Giants visited each of the weak western teams in turn, and swept them all. Late in the season, the westerners came into the Polo Grounds and got swept. The problem for the Giants was that the western teams did almost as badly against Brooklyn, Boston, and Philadelphia as they had against New York. The result was that the Giants' streaks really didn't give them the lift in the standings that you might expect. And between streaks, the Giants not only had to play the strong eastern teams, they had a pile of injuries as well.

Brooklyn took the pennant in 1916, but the Giants got it together and became National League champs the next year—without a record winning streak.

⚾ What's the most games a ⚾ pitcher has ever won in a row?

Like so many other things in baseball history, it depends on how you look at it. Carl Hubbell of the New York Giants won 24 in a row over the last half of the 1936 season and on into May 1937. In the American League, Cleveland's Johnny Allen (in 1936–37) and Baltimore's Dave McNally (in 1969–70) both won 17 in a row over two seasons.

But the consecutive game record is usually thought of as a single-season mark. Here, the modern all-time record of 19 belongs to another Giant, Rube Marquard, who set it in 1912. (Yet an-

other New Yorker, Tim Keefe, won 19 in a row, too, back in 1888, when the pitching distance was only fifty feet.) A few years before he set the record, left-hander Marquard had been known as the $11,000 Lemon, because he'd been bought from the minor league Indianapolis team for that sum (the largest ever paid for a minor leaguer up to that point), and then he hadn't immediately produced. But he'd won 24 games in 1911, and he came back to win 26 in 1912. The Giants won the National League pennant both years.

Strangely, the American League record was set in the same year—by two men. First, Walter Johnson swept through the league, winning 16 in a row before losing. Then Boston's Smokey Joe Wood began a streak of his own. With Wood at 15 wins, he faced Johnson and the Washington Senators at Fenway Park in one of the most famous games in baseball history. The two great fastballers were both superb, and Wood beat Johnson only when one of the Senators made an error. Wood lost his next game, so he and Johnson share the AL record. Johnson went on to a record of 32–12 that year. Wood was even better, with an incredible 34–5.

The American League record was later tied by Lefty Grove of the Athletics in 1931, and the Tigers' Schoolboy Rowe in 1934, both seasons when their teams won the pennant but lost the World Series. Back in 1912, though, Wood's Red Sox defeated Marquard's Giants in the Fall Classic. Wood won three of his team's four victories and was responsible for one loss. Marquard pitched even

Rube Marquard of the Giants won his first 19 decisions in 1912.

better, though not as much. He was 2–0 in the Series, with a 0.50 earned run average.

Not a bad year for pitching, 1912.

Has there ever been a woman in the big leagues?

Not yet. But I wouldn't bet that it will never happen. It's only been in the last few years that girls have been encouraged—or even allowed—to play baseball as kids.

Back in the 1940s and early 1950s, there was an organization called the All-American Girls' Professional Baseball League. The league was set up by Phil Wrigley, who owned the Chicago Cubs. Wrigley was worried that major league ball might be canceled during World War II, and he wanted to be able to move something in to replace it if necessary. The women who joined this league originally were softball players, and they had to convert to hardball. By the '50s, they were playing regular baseball but with slightly shorter distances between the bases and from the pitching rubber to home plate.

The league was full of great athletes and wonderful ballplayers. Wally Pipp, who had played first base for the New York Yankees before Lou Gehrig, called Dorothy Kamenshek the "fanciest fielding first baseman I've ever seen, man or woman."

Over the years women have occasionally had a chance to try their skills against men during exhibition games. The famous Olympian and professional golfer Babe Didriksen pitched against big leaguers. And back in 1931, Jackie Mitchell, a 17-year-old girl from Chattanooga, Tennessee, pitched a few innings for the Chattanooga Lookouts against the New York Yankees, who were barnstorming their way north after spring training. Jackie had a very good sinker, and she used it to strike out Babe Ruth and Lou Gehrig.

Mitchell had signed a contract with the Lookouts, but Commissioner of Baseball Kennesaw Mountain Landis soon proclaimed that he would not sanction such an agreement. Landis, like many people at that time, thought it simply wouldn't be proper for a young woman to play a "man's" sport. Mitchell did, however, tour the south for several years, pitching in exhibitions against minor league teams.

These days, the best woman ballplayers are back to playing softball. In the early '60s, I saw the great Joan Joyce—maybe the best woman softball pitcher ever—strike out Ted Williams on what I recall as four pitched balls. I think he fouled one off. Williams, of course, wasn't used to seeing a ball come from underneath, nor was he used to hitting against someone throwing from softball distance, but if you'd ever seen Joyce's slingshot fastball, you'd have no doubt that she could have been great at baseball—or almost any other sport you could name.

Will there ever be a woman in the big leagues? Who knows? The important thing is that young girls—just like young boys—get the chance to go as far as they can in the sport.

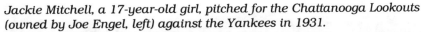

Jackie Mitchell, a 17-year-old girl, pitched for the Chattanooga Lookouts (owned by Joe Engel, left) against the Yankees in 1931.

⚾ *What's the longest anyone* ⚾
has ever played in the majors?

Technically, the man who played major league baseball for the most seasons is a real old-timer named Deacon McGuire. He appeared in games over 26 years from 1884 to 1912. But in the last few of those years, McGuire was the manager of the Red Sox and the Cleveland Naps, and he put himself into only one game a year. McGuire, a catcher, had bounced around his whole career—twelve teams in three leagues—and was never considered a great player.

Eddie Collins, on the other hand, was. Collins holds the American League record for seasons played. He toiled for the Philadelphia Athletics and the Chicago White Sox from 1906 through 1930—25 seasons. He was one of the two or three greatest second basemen in history, a fine spray hitter and a wonderful baserunner. His last three years were a little light on action too. He was a coach for A's manager Connie Mack, and he came to bat almost purely as a pinch hitter. By 1930, he was down to two plate appearances in three games. When he finally retired from the playing field, Collins went into front office work, and he eventually became the general manager of the Boston Red Sox.

In the National League, Pete Rose played in 24 seasons.

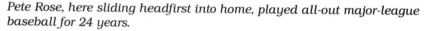

Pete Rose, here sliding headfirst into home, played all-out major-league baseball for 24 years.

⚾ *Who was the youngest player in the majors?* ⚾

There have been lots of young phenoms throughout baseball history. Scads of players have come up when they were 18 or 19. A fair number have even stepped on big league diamonds when they were only 17. But the youngest person to play major league ball in this century was Joe Nuxhall of the Cincinnati Reds, and he was younger than most American Legion players are today. Nuxhall was only 15 when he was sent to the mound on June 10, 1944. Nervous, he walked five men and lasted only two thirds of an inning.

Nuxhall only got his chance as a youngster because most front-line players were away in the service during World War II. He didn't get another opportunity until 1952, when he returned to the mound for the Reds at the more reasonable age of 23. He went on to have a pretty good career, mostly with the Reds, for whom he's now a broadcaster.

In 1887, the Philadelphia Athletics sent a lad named Fred Chapman to the

Joe Nuxhall made his debut with the Cincinnati Reds at the age of 15.

pitcher's box for what turned out to be his first and last big league appearance. His age—14!

⚾ *Who was the oldest* ⚾ *player in the big leagues?*

In baseball, age is a funny thing. A player over 30 is getting along, one over 35 is aging seriously, and anybody in his forties—an age when people in other lines of work are just beginning to hit their strides—is ancient.

Nonetheless, many players have continued to play into their forties. Ty Cobb, for example, didn't quit until he was 41. More recently, Carl Yastrzemski bowed out at the age of 44. Knuckleballers Hoyt Wilhelm and Phil Niekro didn't stop trying to get batters out until they were 49.

But a few players have gone beyond even Wilhelm, to make at least one appearance during their *fifties*. Way back in 1904, Orator Jim O'Rourke, a longtime favorite of the New York fans, went 2 for 4 while catching a complete game for John McGraw's Giants at the age of 52.

I'm not sure what McGraw had in mind when he wrote O'Rourke's name into the lineup, but the three men who appeared in games when they were even older than O'Rourke were participating in gimmicks of one sort or another.

In 1933, the baseball clown and former pitcher Nick Altrock, then 57, was sent up to pinch-hit for Washington at the tail end of the Senator's pennant-winning season. He didn't get a hit.

In 1980, the White Sox twice sent Minnie Minoso up as a pinch hitter when he was also 57. Minnie's career had started in 1949. He'd been a great favorite in Chicago during the '50s and '60s, and the idea here was to give him a chance to play in five different decades, something no one else had ever done. Minoso didn't get a hit, either.

But the all-time champ of the old-timers is the great Satchel Paige, who made his professional debut in 1926, and who may have been the best pitcher anywhere back in the 1930s but who wasn't allowed to play big league ball because he was black. Satch finally came up to the majors as a 42-year-old rookie in 1948, and he hurled effectively for the Cleveland Indians and St. Louis Browns until 1953. Twelve years later, when Paige was 59, Charlie Finley of the then Kansas City A's signed him up and sent him out to start a late-season game. Satch went three innings, allowed one hit, no walks, no runs, and struck out a batter. Not too shabby for an old guy, huh?

⚾ What's the most hits anybody's ⚾ ever gotten in a row in the big leagues?

You know that in baseball, 4 for 4 is an awfully good day, right? Well, how would 12 for 12 sound to you? That's what Mike "Pinky" Higgins of the Red Sox managed over a four-game span in 1938. Higgins, a third baseman, had a pretty good career with the A's, Boston, and the Tigers, and later became manager of the Sox.

Higgins's record was tied by Walt "Moose" Dropo in 1952, just after Boston had traded him to the Tigers. Several years before, Dropo had broken in with a great rookie season in which he'd knocked in 144 runs for the Red Sox.

In the National League, the record is 10 hits in a row, held by eight men, including some of the real greats: Big Ed Delahanty did it for the Phillies in 1897, and Jake Gettman did it for Washington that same year. In 1919, another Big Ed—Ed Konetchy—turned the trick for Brooklyn. KiKi Cuyler of the Pirates did it in 1925, and Chick Hafey did it in 1929, when he was with the Cardinals. Joe "Ducky" Medwick got ten straight with the Cards in 1936. Buddy Hassett of the Boston Braves did it in 1940. And Woody Williams turned the trick for the Reds in 1943. Delahanty, Hafey, Cuyler, and Medwick are all in Baseball's Hall of Fame.

Actually, the most amazing record of this type may belong to the great Ted Williams, who holds the mark for reaching base safely. Over a six-game span in 1957, when he batted .388, Williams got on base *sixteen* times in a row. He was hit by the pitcher once, drew nine walks, rapped two singles, and blasted four home runs. A pretty good week's work.

What's the longest team losing streak in major league history?

Well, back in 1889, the truly terrible Louisville team of the American Association dropped 26 in a row from late May to late June. Not surprisingly, Louisville finished last in the Association that year, 66 games behind the champion Brooklyn club.

Ten years later, the 1899 Cleveland Spiders, arguably the worst big league team of all time, lost 24 consecutive games toward the end of a catastrophic season in which they finished 84 games off the pace set by yet another Brooklyn team. The so-called "modern" National League record is held by the 1961 Phillies, who dropped 23 straight.

In the American League, the futility record is held by the Baltimore Orioles, who opened the 1988 season with 22 consecutive losses. Before that epic feat, the mark had been shared by the Red Sox of 1906 and the Athletics of both 1916 and 1943, each of which had lost 20 in a row.

Long losing streaks are depressing enough, but for a really concerted blow to the spirit, try this. During the 1928 season, the Boston Braves lost both ends of five doubleheaders—all in a week's time. Seven years before, the Braves' crosstown partners in crime, the Red Sox, had done almost as badly. In seven days, they lost four doubleheaders. Pity those Beantown fans.

What does "slugging average" mean?

Here's what the rule book says: "To compute slugging percentage, divide the total bases of all safe hits by the total times at bat. . . ."

What for? Well, the idea is that if you give a batter credit for his total bases, you'll come up with a pretty good measurement of how good a power hitter he is. But to register a high slugging average, a batter has to have a pretty good batting average, along with a lot of extra-base hits. For example, in 1982, Dave Kingman hit a league-leading 37 home runs for the New York Mets. But he only batted .204, and because he made so many outs, his slugging average was just .432. In 1979, on the other hand, Kingman had batted .288 for the Cubs while leading the league with 48 homers. His slugging average that year was .613.

Not surprisingly, Babe Ruth has the highest lifetime slugging average in baseball history. His .690 puts him ahead of Ted Williams and Lou Gehrig, the only other two men over .600 lifetime. Ruth also holds nine of the top eleven seasonal slugging averages. His incredible .847 in 1920—the year he hit 54 home runs—is the best ever.

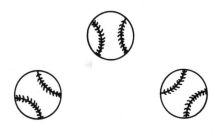

⚾ I read somewhere that the Commissioner of ⚾ Baseball decided that Roger Maris's 61 home runs would have an asterisk next to it in the record books, but I've never seen it. Why?

You're right. In 1961, the American League had expanded from eight teams to ten, and from 154 games in a season to 162. Many fans were seriously worried that the longer season would give modern players an unfair advantage in breaking baseball records.

Their concerns seemed reasonable when both Maris and Mickey Mantle mounted serious assaults on what was then baseball's most hallowed record—Babe Ruth's 60 homers in a season.

In those days, the Commissioner of Baseball was a man named Ford Frick. Commissioner Frick had been a New York newspaper writer during Ruth's glory years, and had been a close friend of the Babe. As the season progressed and neither Mantle nor Maris dropped off the pace, Frick announced that Ruth's record had to be broken in 154 games, or it would go into the books with an asterisk (*) next to it so that everyone would know it was set in a longer season.

As it turned out, Maris didn't get his 60th home run until the 159th game of the season. His 61st came in the 163rd game (the Yanks played 163 because they had played a tie back in April). So Frick proclaimed that the record would be listed with an asterisk.

Almost right away, though, people began raising objections. In the first place, although it had come in game 159, Maris's 60th homer had come in three fewer times at bat than Ruth's had in 1927. Besides, many fans thought, a season record was a season record. Adjustments couldn't be made every time the league's schedule changed or a team had to play an extra game or two.

This point was well made the next year, when Maury Wills was attacking Ty Cobb's single-season record for stolen bases. The National League had expanded that year and had joined the American League in adopting a 162-game schedule. As Wills began to run wild, Frick ruled that he'd have to break Cobb's mark of 96 stolen bases in 154 games, or Wills, too, would suffer the asterisk penalty. It turned out, though, that Cobb had actually played 156 games back in 1915, so Commissioner Frick had to adjust his thinking. Wills got his 97th stolen base in his 156th game, so no asterisk was applied. He eventually ran his total up to 104.

When the Macmillan *Baseball Ency-*

Roger Maris hit a record 61 home runs in 1961.

clopedia first came out back in the late '60s, its editors stated that they were treating all season records alike: no asterisks. And that's the way pretty much everyone has handled things. There may be some sort of "official" listing somewhere that actually includes the asterisk next to Maris's name, but I've never seen one—and I bet you never will, either. We're used to the 162-game season these days, and we realize that great seasons by modern players like Maris and Wills don't tarnish in the least the greatness of giants like Ruth and Cobb.

⚾ Has a pitcher ever won ⚾ both games of a doubleheader?

Sure, lots of times. But not for many years. The best-known pitcher to do it was Cy Young, who won a pair for Cleveland in 1890, his rookie season. Grover Cleveland Alexander did it twice, in 1916 and 1917. But it hasn't been done by anyone since Dutch Levsen managed it for the Indians in 1926.

The most remarkable performance along these lines was turned in by Joe McGinnity of the 1903 New York Giants. He won both ends of a doubleheader *three* times that season. In fact, all three twin bills were played in the space of three weeks. McGinnity was a hard-nosed submarine pitcher who—not surprisingly—led the National League in both victories (31) and innings pitched (434) that year. It was performances like this that earned him the nickname he's known by even today: Iron Man.

Modern pitchers just don't do this sort of thing. Teams carry more pitchers on their rosters today, and managers don't want to run the risk of ruining valuable arms by overworking them. Most teams establish a five-man rotation that has each starter working a game every four days. Only under extreme circumstances will a pitcher these days even come back a day early, let alone pitch two games in a day. I don't blame them at all. But I *am* sorry we'll never have a pitcher nicknamed Iron Man again!

Iron Man Joe McGinnity won both ends of a doubleheader three times in one year!

What was the longest game in big league history?

You're talking here about one of the all-time great pitching duels. On May 1, 1920, Joe Oeschger of the Boston Braves went to the mound against Brooklyn, whose starter was Leon Cadore.

Both pitchers were on, and they both pitched shutout ball for four innings. The Dodgers scored in the top of the fifth, and the Braves came back to tie the game in the bottom of the sixth.

From that point on, neither pitcher gave the batters anything. The 1–1 tie extended through the ninth and into extra innings. Through the twelfth, the fifteenth, the twentieth, the twenty-fifth. Finally, after the twenty-sixth inning, umpire Barry McCormick called the game on account of darkness. It ended a 1–1 tie.

If the game had gone one more inning in length, it would have equaled three regular games. Cadore had pitched to 95 batters, giving up 15 hits. Oeschger had faced 85 and yielded 9 basehits.

To modern fans, one of the most amazing things about this longest of all games is that it took only three hours and fifty minutes. We've seen regular nine-inning games take that long.

Despite their marvelous performances on this day, neither Cadore nor Oeschger is remembered as a great pitcher. Cadore's record for ten years in the big leagues was only 68–72. Oeschger ended up 83–116. But on May 1, 1920, they were both about as good as a pitcher can be. Neither of them got to chalk up a win, but they both earned more lasting fame for this monster tie than they did for all the games either one of them won during the rest of their careers.

Who was the first real relief pitcher?

The relief pitcher has only recently become absolutely essential to a team's success. For many years in baseball's early days, pitchers almost always finished their games, even when they were being pounded. Clubs only carried a couple of hurlers, and some of them rang up astonishing numbers because they pitched so often.

Later, pitching staffs grew, and managers would make a change if they really had to. But the men coming out of the bullpen were often regular starters being called upon in an emergency.

The first well-known pitcher who was used primarily in relief was Fred "Firpo" Marberry of the Washington Senators.

Manager Bucky Harris brought him in from the pen a total of ninety times during Washington's pennant years of 1924 and 1925. "Saves" wasn't an official record category in those days, but applying current standards, Marberry led the American League in saves five times from 1924 to 1932, with totals ranging from 11 to 22.

At roughly the same time, the Yankees had Wilcy Moore, who led the league with 13 saves in 1927. Moore moved along to Boston, where he led the league once more with 10 saves in 1931.

Johnny Murphy picked up where Marberry and Moore left off, saving games for the Yankees through the late

'30s and early '40s. He was succeeded by Joe Page as the Yankee's big fireman.

In the mid-'50s, Ray Narleski and Don Mossi formed a potent left-right team coming out of the Cleveland Indian bullpen. In the National League at the same time, the Dodgers' Clem Labine always seemed to be trudging slowly out of the pen to nail down another Brooklyn victory. When the Dodgers moved to Los Angeles, Labine was succeeded by Larry Sherry, then Ron Perranoski.

Back in the American League, the Yankees came up with the fireballing Ryne Duren, then Luis Arroyo, master of the screwball. The Red Sox discovered Dick Radatz, the Monster.

These days, there are more big-name relievers in the majors than there were all together up to 1970 or so. You could make the argument that nothing—not night baseball, not the designated hitter, not artificial turf—has changed the game more than a Rollie Fingers or Goose Gossage or Tom Henke waiting for the call and then strolling in to shut down a late-inning rally. Bucky Harris

Fred "Firpo" Marberry was a great reliever for the Washington Senators and Detroit Tigers.

sure had the right idea with Firpo Marberry. It just took a while to sink in.

⚾ Beside Roger Maris, what player ⚾ came closest to Babe Ruth's record of 60 home runs in a season?

There's a famous trick answer to this question: Babe Ruth. The Babe himself hit 59 homers in 1921. Until Maris came along forty years later, no one else got that close.

But a few other great sluggers had good runs at Ruth's record. The most unlikely challenger was the Chicago Cubs' Hack Wilson. Wilson stood only five feet six inches, and he had tiny feet, size 5½. But he weighed a hundred and ninety pounds and was built like a fireplug (in fact, he was sometimes referred to as the Hardest-hitting Hydrant of All Time). He was a terrible outfielder, but during the late '20s and early '30s, he was one of the National League's premier sluggers. In 1930, he had one of the great offensive seasons of all time. He slammed 56 home runs, which remains today the National League record. Even more remarkable is the fact that along with those homers, he registered 190 runs batted in. No one—not Ruth, not Gehrig, not anybody—ever drove in more.

Two years later, back in the American League, Jimmie Foxx, the ferociously strong Philadelphia A's first baseman, blasted 58 homers. It was the first time in seven years that anyone but the Babe had won the AL home-run championship. Unlike Wilson, Foxx was a big man with big muscles—he *looked* like a slugger. Foxx, too, got a lot of mileage out of his homers. He drove in 169 that year. Curiously, after winning three straight pennants, the A's fell back to second in 1932, despite Foxx's big run production.

A few years later, in 1938, Hank Greenberg duplicated Foxx's feat. The Detroit Tiger first baseman hit 58 homers, driving in 144 runs. Greenberg later became one of the many players whose careers were interrupted by World War II. When he left for the service, he had 249 career home runs. He spent more than four years in the Army, and then, on his first day back with the Tigers, finally hit his 250th round-tripper.

Aside from Wilson, Foxx, and Greenberg, the closest anyone (besides Maris and Ruth, of course) has gotten to 60 in a season is 54. Ruth himself did that twice, in 1920 and 1928. And Mickey Mantle reached that level in 1961, the year Maris finally broke the mark. (Not surprisingly, Mantle's and Maris's combined 115 home runs is the most ever by two teammates in the same sea-

In 1930 Hack Wilson of the Chicago Cubs hit a National League record 56 home runs, and drove in an incredible 190 runs.

son.) Over in the National League, Ralph Kiner hit 54 for the Pirates in 1949.

Very few other players have ever hit as many as 50 home runs. Foxx, Kiner, and Mantle each managed it one more time. George Foster, Johnny Mize, and Willie Mays each did it once. That's it.

Many of these men were ahead of Ruth's pace for much of the season. One of the most remarkable things about the Babe's 1927 record, and the element that only Roger Maris has been able to overcome, is the fact that he went into September with "only" 43 homers, and hit an amazing 17 during the season's last month.

⚾ *What does it mean to "hit for the cycle"?* ⚾

A player who hits for the cycle gets one of each kind of hit (single, double, triple, home run) during a single game. It's a pretty rare event that happens only about once each season in each league. What stymies most players is the triple, which is the hardest hit to get, because it calls for a combination of power and speed.

The record for hitting for the cycle is three times, and it's shared by three men. The first to manage it was Long John Reilly, a real old-timer who did it twice in 1883 for the Cincinnati team of the American Association, and once in 1890 for Cincinnati's National League club.

Outfielder Bob Meusel did it three times for the Yankees during the '20s. Meusel was a teammate of Babe Ruth and a pretty good slugger in his own right—he led the league in home runs in 1925, when the Babe came down with his famous stomach ache that reduced him to playing in only 98 games.

Finally, Babe Herman hit for the cycle three times during his years in the National League, twice for the Dodgers in 1931, then once two years later for the Cubs. Herman was a great Brooklyn favorite whose weak play in the outfield was offset by his great bat. In 1930, he hit .393, but he didn't win the batting title because that was the year Bill Terry of the Giants hit .401.

The only player to hit for the cycle in both the American and National leagues is Bob Watson, who did it for both the Houston Astros and the Boston Red Sox. Watson is also the man credited with scoring the National League's one millionth run while he was with the Astros.

Bob Meusel hit for the cycle on three occasions.

⚾ What team has won the ⚾ most pennants and World Series?

When I was a kid, it was big news when the New York Yankees *didn't* win the American League pennant. This was true from the early 1920s all the way into the mid-1960s. In fact, from 1921 through 1964, the Yanks won the flag almost two thirds of the time—28 league championships in 44 years. And they had 19 World Series victories over that time too.

You can roughly break the great Yankee years into three periods: the era of Miller Huggins, the era of Joe McCarthy, and the era of Casey Stengel. Each of these managers led New York to at least eight pennants, and each is in the Baseball Hall of Fame for his efforts.

In 1921, the Yankees won their first pennant under Huggins. In those days, the Giants were the best-loved and most successful team in the city. The two teams met in the first of many "subway Series" (actually, the Polo Grounds was the home park of both in 1921–22), and the Giants, in their seventh autumn classic, won the world championship. The same thing happened the following year. In 1923, the two teams met for the third straight time, and this time the Yankees—now in their own Yankee stadium—triumphed, finally winning their first Series after two decades in the league. Ironically, one of the two games the Giants took that year was won on an inside-the-park home run hit by their aging left fielder—a popular former dental student named Casey Stengel.

After two off-years, the Yankees came back to win the pennant in 1926, but lost the Series to the St. Louis Cardinals. The seventh game of this series witnessed one of the legendary pitching performances of all time. With the Cardinals leading 3–2 in the seventh, the Yankees loaded the bases with two out, and the dangerous Tony Lazzeri up. Playing manager Rogers Hornsby called old Grover Cleveland Alexander in from the bullpen. Alexander had already won two games for the Cards in the Series, including game six. He didn't expect to be asked to pitch in game seven. Some say he was sleeping off a hangover. But in he came, the ultimate old pro, to whiff Lazzeri under incredible pressure and save the lead. In the ninth, a possible Yankee rally was snuffed out, and the Series lost, when Babe Ruth, of all people, was thrown out trying to steal second base with two outs.

The Yankees won two more pennants (and World Series) under Huggins, but the little man died in 1929. In the early '30s, Joe McCarthy took over the team. New York won the pennant and Series in 1932, then settled for second until 1936. From that point through 1943, they won seven more pennants and six World Series. This was the team dominated by Joe DiMaggio but loaded with other great players: catcher Bill Dickey, first baseman (until May 1939) Lou Gehrig, Frank Crosetti, Red Rolfe, Tommy Henrich, Joe Gordon, Charlie Keller, the young Phil Rizzuto, and pitchers like Lefty Gomez and Red Ruffing. Some think this was the greatest Yankee era of all.

After World War II, New York took a pennant and a Series under Bucky Harris. In 1949, Casey Stengel took over the team. Stengel had managed several teams in the National League without much success, but with the Yankees, his team won the pennant and the Series that year, and again the next, and the next, and the next, and the next. It was the first time in baseball history that a team had won five straight pennants, let alone five straight World Championships. They slipped in 1954, with a "mere" 103 wins to the Indians' 111. But they were back in 1955, and between then and 1964, they lost the pennant only twice, though they won the Series "only" four times. It was under Stengel that Don Larsen pitched his perfect game against Brooklyn in the 1956 World Series. It was also under Stengel that the Yankees lost the Series to Pittsburgh in 1960, when Bill Mazeroski hit a dramatic homer in the last inning of the seventh game. From 1960 through 1964, the Yankees once again won the pennant five straight times: one was won under Stengel, three under his successor Ralph Houk, and one under Yogi Berra. Berra had played for the Yankees in a record fourteen Series from 1947 through 1963—an amazing total of 75 games.

Where Ruth had been the big name on the clubs of the '20s and early '30s, and DiMaggio had been the big man on the teams of the late '30s and '40s,

Casey Stengel piloted the Yankees to ten pennants in twelve years, including five consecutive World's Championships.

these Yankee teams of the '50s and '60s were Mickey Mantle's. Like the other two great slugging outfielders, though, he had plenty of help: Berra, Gil McDougald, Hank Bauer, Bill Skowron, Elston Howard, Tony Kubek, Bobby Richardson, Roger Maris, Allie Reynolds, Vic Raschi, Eddie Lopat, Whitey Ford, Bob Turley.

Since '64, the Yankees have had their ups and downs. They fell all the way to the cellar in 1966, and remained pretty bad until the mid-1970s. Then they went on another binge. From 1976 through 1981, they won five Eastern Division championships, four American League pennants, and three World Series. Unlike the other eras of Yankee greatness, though, this one was typified by arguments and upheaval, not solidity and continuity. And it was an era that has to be named after an owner, not a manager. It was the era of George Steinbrenner.

The Yankees will certainly be back to win more pennants and championships, but they'll never dominate the game as they once did. Neither will anyone else.

⚾ *Has there ever been a tripleheader?* ⚾

Boy, most players would tell you that playing a couple of games in a day is plenty! Actually, though, there was a tripleheader played between Cincinnati and Pittsburgh back in 1920. Late in the season, the Reds were in third, and the Pirates were in fourth, three and a half games out of third place with only four games to play. As A. D. Suehsdorf wrote in an article on the subject, the Pittsburgh players wanted badly to make it into third place so that they could collect a small share of the upcoming World Series' gate receipts. A four-game sweep of Cincinnati would do the trick.

Unfortunately for the Pirates, the first of their four-game set with the Reds rained out. Normally, the game wouldn't have been made up, because it had no effect on the race for first place. That would ruin Pittsburgh's hope for a shot at third, because they'd be three and a half back with only three more to play.

But the Pirates' owner got the president of the National League to declare that the teams would play a tripleheader the next day, October 2, rather than the scheduled doubleheader, thus giving the Pirates a shot at third-place money.

It did no good. The Reds ruined Pittsburgh's hopes right away, winning the first game 13–4. They played a lineup of substitutes and pitchers in the second game but won again, anyway, 7–3. Finally, the Pirates took one, winning the third game, which was called on account of darkness after six innings, 6–0.

The three games took exactly five hours to play—2:03 for the first, 1:56 for the second, and 1:01 for the shortened third. These days, a doubleheader takes longer than that.

Tripleheaders also took place on September 1, 1890 between Pittsburgh (again!) and Brooklyn, and on September 7, 1896 between Baltimore and Louisville; all three of the tripleheaders ever played occurred in the National League.

70

Baseball has had its share of speedsters, but there's no sure way to know which one was the quickest. My guess, though, is that if you were somehow able to arrange a hundred-yard dash among the fastest men who ever wore big league uniforms, you'd want to put your money on Herb Washington.

That's too bad, because Washington, who was with Charlie Finley's Oakland A's for a couple of years in the mid-'70s, wasn't really a ballplayer. Washington *was* a world-class hurdler with blinding speed, though, and Finley thought he could use him effectively as a "designated runner." So Washington appeared in a total of 104 games, always as a pinch runner. He never got to swing a bat or chase down a drive in the outfield. And he never really got the hang of running the bases, either, although he stole 28 bases in 1974. The clearest memory many people have of Washington is of seeing him picked off first base by Mike Marshall of the Dodgers during the 1974 World Series.

Washington may have been the all-time flat-out speedster, but there are probably more truly fast runners in baseball today than there ever have been at one time before. For one thing, players in general are simply bigger, stronger, and quicker than they were in years past. And with all the artificial-turf ballparks around now, the emphasis on many teams has turned from power to speed. Scouts and managers value quickness more highly than they used to, so more real burners get drafted and encouraged through the minors. Guys like Vince Coleman, Rickey Henderson, and Tim Raines are about as quick on the bases as anyone's ever been. A few years ago, so was Willie Wilson.

Youngsters are sometimes surprised to hear that Mickey Mantle was once considered the fastest man in the game. It's unusual for sluggers to be sprinters as well, but when Mantle first came up, many old-timers said he was the quickest who ever played the game. Mickey hurt his leg early in his career, and he was never quite the bolt of lightning he had been, but he remained for a number of years the consensus pick as fastest man in the American League.

Cool Papa Bell played in the Negro Leagues in the years before black players were allowed into the National and American Leagues. He was perhaps the fastest of the many fast black players who never had the chance to play in front of big major league crowds. Cool Papa was so fast, said his roommate Satchel Paige, "that he could turn out the light and jump into bed before it got dark."

James "Cool Papa" Bell may have been the fastest baserunner of all.

My favorite old-time speedster is a man called Harry Bay, who played big league ball for the Reds and the Indians from 1901 through 1908. Bay led his league in stolen bases only once, but he was famously fast and earned the nickname Deerfoot from other players and the press. In guides and children's books of the era, it's often Deerfoot Harry Bay who is singled out as the baserunner to emulate. I love that nickname. It's gentle and smooth, and it tells you what you need to know about Mr. Bay.

The great Olympian Jim Thorpe played some major league ball during the teens. Thorpe was undoubtedly one of the fastest men in the game during that period, but his world-level success on the track was not as a sprinter, and he probably wouldn't register with the quickest players of all time.

Fast players are best recognized in eras when the running game is important. Most of the speedsters of the '30s, '40s, and '50s got relatively little notice, because the game in those years was based largely on power and the home run. Stolen base totals were generally lower than they had been in earlier years or were to become later. But pure speed, either on the basepaths or in the outfield, has always been one of the flashiest and most enjoyable parts of the game. We're lucky to be able to see so much of it in action today.

Is it true that someone once caught a ball dropped from the Washington Monument?

Yup. It was done in 1894 by Chicago catcher Pop Schriver, then again in 1908 by Gabby Street, who was Walter Johnson's backstop with the Washington Senators. Handling the Big Train's fastball was probably the best preparation Street could have gotten for his stunt.

The balls Schriver and Street caught fell 505 feet, but another catcher grabbed one that had been dropped from an even higher building. In 1940, Hank Helf, a reserve catcher for the Indians, caught a ball dropped 700 feet from the top of the Terminal Tower in Cleveland.

Back in 1930, Joe Sprinz, who was another reserve Cleveland catcher (what is it with these guys?) caught a ball tossed not off a building, but out of a blimp cruising at 800 feet. Sprinz held on, but the force of the shock broke his jaw.

I can't find out positively, but I think all four of these catchers were wearing their masks and chest protectors when they made their catches.

I know for sure that Wilbert Robinson was wearing the gear when he tried to make a similar catch in what turned out to be one of baseball's funniest off-the-field episodes. Uncle Robbie was then managing the Dodgers, and during spring training in 1916, he agreed to try to catch a ball dropped out of an airplane circling the practice field.

Unbeknownst to Robinson, Casey Stengel, then playing for the Dodgers, had given a grapefruit to Brooklyn equipment manager Dan Comerford, who was doing the dropping. Comerford tossed out the grapefruit, and Robbie, on the ground below, started circling to get into position. He yelled, "I got it! I got it!" to keep other players away, and then he settled in to make the catch.

Kaboom! The grapefruit exploded

Gabby Street was one of two men ever to catch a ball dropped from the top of the Washington Monument.

into Robinson's mitt and knocked him down, spraying juice and pulp all over him. Robinson felt the gooey liquid on his face and hands and started yelling, "Help, help! I'm bleeding to death!" The other players, of course, were doubled over with laughter. Babe Herman said that for years afterward, many of them called their manager Grapefruit. I wonder what Grapefruit called Casey Stengel when he found out what had really happened.

⚾ *What are the best baseball books?* ⚾

As fans, we're lucky that our favorite sport has had so much wonderful stuff written about it. There are dozens of fine baseball books covering history, statistics, and personalities—all areas of the game. Which ones are best is a matter of personal choice, but here are a few I think you might enjoy.

The books that I enjoyed most as a kid were the *Fireside* books, edited by Charles Einstein. The first three are out of print, though some of their pieces are grouped in a volume called *The Baseball Reader*. A new fourth volume is available. The wonderful thing about these books is that Einstein has combined all different kinds of fine and interesting writing about the game. Reading even a single volume will give you an idea of the sweep, history, great moments, and characters of baseball. Most of the pieces are short, and there are lots of pictures. You can dip in to read for a few minutes and then go off to something else. Great stuff.

Back in the '60s, a man named Lawrence Ritter drove around the country and interviewed old men who had played big league ball in the early part of the century. Then he put together a wonderful book of their memories called *The Glory of Their Times*. Read it and you can hear men who played with and against them talking about players like Ty Cobb and Honus Wagner and Tris Speaker. Many people call this their favorite baseball book.

If you're really interested in the details of players' careers, you'll want access to Macmillan's *Baseball Encyclopedia*. It is quite expensive ($40 or more), but many libraries have it. The book lists the record of every man who's ever played in the big leagues and gives a lot of information about the World Series and all-time records as well.

Statistics like this are important to baseball, and if you'd like to see how they are used by experts, you should check out *The Hidden Game of Baseball* by Pete Palmer and John Thorn, or the annual *Elias Baseball Analyst* by Seymour Siwoff and the Hirdt brothers. Some people get annoyed by the way these writers approach baseball, because they question standard ideas and points of view. But I think you might find their conclusions pretty interesting.

If you're a ballplayer yourself, there are two books on hitting that even big leaguers have found helpful. The first is Ted Williams's *The Science of Hitting*, and the other is Charlie Lau's *The Art of Hitting .300*. Williams, of course, was one of the game's great hitters, and one of the neat things about his book is a chart that shows how well he could hit pitches in different parts of the strike zone. Lau was just a journeyman catcher, but he was George Brett's hitting coach, and his ideas influence the way many fine current hitters—Wade Boggs, Don Mattingly, Tony Gwynn—swing the bat.

Finally, a really terrific book that helps make sense of the baseball rule book is *Baseball By the Rules* by Glen Waggoner, Kathleen Moloney, and Hugh Howard. The authors don't just repeat the rules to you, they show you how they work by using real big league plays and events.

As I said, there are dozens of wonderful baseball books out there. I've only mentioned a few, but your public library will probably have a pretty good selection. Baseball would be a great game if nobody ever wrote a word about it, but what a wonderful bonus all this great reading is!

What, exactly, is the "triple crown"?

A player wins the triple crown if he leads his league in batting average, home runs, and runs batted in—all in a single season. As you might expect, this doesn't happen very often.

The first player to pull it off in this century—although it wasn't recognized as the triple crown back then—was Ty Cobb, in 1909. He hit .377, drove in 115 runs, and hit 9—yes, 9—home runs. This was the dead-ball era, don't forget.

A few years later, Heinie Zimmerman

of the Cubs did the same thing in the National League. In 1912, he batted .372, knocked in 98, and hit 14 homers.

The first triple crown player with what we'd consider modern power statistics was Rogers Hornsby in 1922 (.401, 152, and 42). Three years later, Hornsby became the first player to win the crown twice, when he batted .403 with 143 RBIs and 39 home runs.

In 1933, both leagues—for the only time in history—had triple crown win-

Rogers Hornsby won the triple crown twice—in 1922 and 1925.

ners in the same year. In the National League, Check Klein of the Phillies hit .368 and had 120 RBIs and 28 round-trippers. At the same time, another Philadelphia player, Jimmie Foxx of the Athletics, was ringing up a .356 average, 163 RBIs, and 48 homers.

Lou Gehrig won the American League's triple crown the next year (.363, 165, 49), and Joe Medwick did it for the Cardinals in 1937 (.374, 154, 31). That's the last time any National League hitter has put it all together in one season.

During the '40s, though, Ted Williams of the Boston Red Sox joined Hornsby as a two-time triple crown winner. In 1942, he hit .356 with 137 RBIs and 36 home runs. Five years later, after returning from World War II, Williams did it again (.343, 114, 32.)

The Yankees' Mickey Mantle led the pack in all three categories in 1956 (.353, 130, 52), and then it was ten more years before anyone could do it again. Then two players managed it in consecutive seasons: The Orioles' Frank Robinson hit .316 with 122 RBIs and 49 home runs in 1966, and the Red Sox's Carl Yastrzemski came back the next year with .326, 121, and 44. No one's won a triple crown since.

The combination of power and average that the triple crown requires has never been common in baseball, and it may be less common than ever today. The '70s was the first decade of the century that saw no one win the honor, and we've yet to see a winner in the '80s.

⚾ *Who were the biggest and smallest players?* ⚾

One of the nice things about baseball is that sheer size—or the lack of it—doesn't have much to do with how good you are at the game. Most of the game's best players have been more or less "normal"-sized—within an inch or two of six feet either way, and neither fat nor skinny. Ty Cobb was 6'1", 175. Roberto Clemente was 5'11", 175. Willie Mays was 5'10 ", 170. Carl Yastrzemski was 5'11", 175.

Of course, there have been players noted almost as much for their size as for their talent. One problem here is that the heights and playing weights listed for ballplayers aren't always accurate, but let's give this one a try.

The biggest man I ever saw on a baseball field was Frank "Hondo" Howard, who played for the Dodgers, the Washington Senators–Texas Rangers, and the Tigers, from 1958 through 1973. Howard stood 6'7" tall and is listed in the *Baseball Encyclopedia* at 255. I bet he weighed a good bit more than that during much of his career. I remember watching Howard standing next to Boog Powell—himself 6'4 ", 230—at an All-Star Game around 1970, and thinking that he made Boog look almost *small.* There may have been a few guys over the years who weighed more than Howard (Walter "Jumbo" Brown of the 1930s Yanks and Giants tipped the scales at 295), and there are a few in the game now who are as tall, but I don't think there was ever a ballplayer as overwhelmingly *large* as Frank Howard.

Back in the 1890s, there was another big man who must have looked almost as imposing to the smaller population of the time as Howard did to me. Roger Connor, known as Old Reliable, was the Hall of Fame first baseman of the New York Giants during the 1880s and '90s. He stood 6'3" and weighed 220 pounds—a real giant in that era.

Connor was a truly extraordinary player whose career record of 136 home runs wasn't broken until Babe Ruth came along.

For a short time, Connor had as a teammate one of baseball's best-known small players. "Wee Willie" Keeler was an outfielder for New York, the famous Baltimore Oriole teams of the '90s, Brooklyn, and finally, the new New York team in the American League. Keeler was a great place hitter who led the National League with a .432 average in 1897, and repeated with a .379 the next year. When someone asked him how he hit so well, he replied, "I keep a clear eye, and I hit 'em where they ain't." Keeler was all of 5'4 " tall, but he had a major league career average of .345—fifth on the all-time list.

Another slight Hall of Famer was Johnny Evers, the second baseman of the famous Tinker-to-Evers-to-Chance

Left: Wee Willer Keeler stood only 5'4½" tall, but that didn't stop him from hitting .345 over a 19-year career. Right: Frank Howard was overwhelmingly large.

double-play combination for the Chicago Cubs. Evers stood a respectable 5'9" tall, but he weighed only 125 pounds during much of his career. Evers, one of the smartest players of his day, was a very nervous type, and he simply couldn't gain weight. In fact, many observers say that late in the season, Evers weighed even less than his featherweight listed poundage.

A few years later in his career, Evers played for the Boston Braves, where his double-play partner was shortstop Rabbit Maranville, another little Hall of Famer. Maranville, known for catching infield pop-ups with the waist-level basket catch Willie Mays would make famous years later, was only 5'5" tall. He and Evers made up what must have been the all-time little-guy keystone combination.

Of course, the smallest man ever to appear in a big league game was the midget Eddie Gaedel, who had one at-bat for the St. Louis Browns against the Detroit Tigers in 1951. He was 3'7" tall and weighed only 65 pounds. Gaedel's strike zone was only a few inches high, and he walked on four pitches. Bill Veeck, owner of the Browns, used Gaedel as a gimmick, and American League President Will Harridge immediately ordered him not to play little Eddie again.

More recently, two of the smallest major leaguers I remember are Albie Pearson and Freddie Patek. (The smallest, Harry Chappas, played sparingly at shortstop for the Chicago White Sox in 1978–80; he was 5'3".) Patek was 5'5", and he held down shortstop for the Kansas City Royals through the '70s. Although Freddie was short, he wasn't especially slight. He had the sturdy neck and thick arms of a linebacker. If you'd seen him apart from other bigger players, you wouldn't have thought, "He looks short." You would have thought, "He looks strong."

Pearson was an outfielder who played with the Washington Senators, the Baltimore Orioles, and the Los Angeles–California Angels from 1958 through 1966. He was 5'5" tall, and he was always showing up in newspaper photos good-naturedly standing under the outstretched arm of some taller teammate, or sitting nestled in somebody's arms. I always thought that Albie, who was a pretty good ballplayer, handled this stuff pretty well. I can imagine what Johnny Evers, whose nickname was the Crab, would have said to a photographer who suggested such a pose.

⚾ *Who was baseball's best manager?* ⚾

There have been many fine managers in baseball history. Two of the best known are John McGraw of the New York Giants and Connie Mack of the Philadelphia Athletics. McGraw led the Giants for 33 years, winning ten pennants and three World Series. Mack managed the A's for an incredible 53 years, racking up nine pennants and five World Championships. The two men met each other in the Series four times (Mack's men won three).

A number of other managers have joined these two men in the Hall of Fame: Walter Alston and Wilbert Robinson of the Dodgers; Miller Huggins, Joe McCarthy, and Casey Stengel of the Yankees; Bucky Harris of the Senators and Tigers; Bill McKechnie of the Pirates, the Cardinals, and the Reds; and others. And there are some wonderful managers who have worked over the last twenty years or so: Earl Weaver and Whitey Herzog are good examples.

But my two favorites are guys you probably never heard of: Frank Selee and George Stallings—and they both managed the same team.

Selee (pronounced *see*-lee) took over the Boston Beaneaters of the National League in 1890 and led them to five pennants during the '90s. The Baltimore Orioles are usually remembered as the great team of that era, but the Orioles took only three flags.

Before he turned Boston into a winner, Selee had to sort out problems on the team and find a number of good new players. Once he got things settled, though, Boston came to be known as the smartest team in baseball. The Beaneaters developed the modern hit-and-run play, and they were the first team to use signals much as modern teams do today.

Why is Selee forgotten today? Probably because the newspapermen of the first three decades of this century focused much of their attention on John McGraw and the Giants. McGraw was a great manager himself, but he had also played for the Baltimore Orioles against Selee's Beaneaters. McGraw told wonderful stories about the old Orioles and gave them credit for many of the things Selee and his Beaneaters actually did.

So Selee, who really belongs in the Hall of Fame, never got the recognition he deserved.

George Stallings took over the Boston team—by then called the Braves—in time for the 1913 season. And what he did the following year earned him forever the nickname Miracle Man. Boston, in the decade after Selee left in 1901, had gotten pretty bad. In fact, they'd finished last in 1909, 1910, 1911, and 1912. Stallings shook them up in 1913, and they finished fifth. But in 1914, the "Miracle" Braves—in last place as late as July 19—astonished the baseball world by taking the National League pennant. And they didn't stop there: they swept four straight from the great Philadelphia A's—winners of three of the last four World Championships—in the Series.

During this great season, Stallings juggled his team as no manager ever had before. He introduced the idea of regularly platooning different players at the same position. Other managers have much better career records than Stallings, but I don't think anyone has ever done a greater job over a single season. The Miracle Man deserves his nickname.

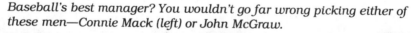

Baseball's best manager? You wouldn't go far wrong picking either of these men—Connie Mack (left) or John McGraw.

Well, I don't know about the *worst,* but there have been some pretty important and famous errors of commission and omission made over the years.

The one you might remember yourself is Bill Buckner's during the 1986 World Series between the Boston Red Sox and the New York Mets. Boston first baseman Buckner let an easy ground ball go right through his legs in the ninth inning of the sixth game. The Mets scored the game-winning run on the play, and they went on to win the World Series two nights later.

Buckner's error reminded a lot of people of the famous "Snodgrass Muff" of the 1912 World Series. The same two cities were involved: the Red Sox were playing the Giants. In the seventh game, Giant center fielder Fred Snodgrass dropped a fly ball in the ninth inning. The man who hit it, Clyde Engle, later scored the game's tying run, and the Red Sox went on to win.

Wild pitches aren't officially errors, but they're close enough to mention a few of them here. In that same '86 Series game, the Red Sox's Bob Stanley uncorked a wild one with two outs in the ninth, two strikes on the batter, and a man on third. The Mets scored the tying run, setting things up for Buckner's miscue.

Eighty-four years earlier, another wild pitch determined the outcome of a pennant race. In 1904, pitcher "Happy Jack" Chesbro of the American League's New York Highlanders won 41 games. But on the final day of the season, he threw a wild pitch that lost a game—and the pennant as well. The Highlanders needed to sweep a last-day doubleheader from Boston to take the flag. Boston needed to win only one to win their second straight championship. The score was tied 2–2 in the ninth

inning of the first game, with a man on third and two outs. Chesbro got a ball and two strikes on shortstop Freddy Parent, then fired a spitball (then a legal pitch). A spitter usually drops, but this one didn't. It sailed over the catcher's head, and the winning run scored for Boston. Chesbro, who won more games in a year than any other pitcher of this century, ended his greatest season as a goat.

Finally, another mistake that wasn't really an error is remembered as the greatest blunder in baseball history. In 1908, Fred Merkle was a nineteen-year-old reserve for John McGraw's New York Giants. With regular first baseman Fred Tenney out with an injury, Merkle was in the lineup on September 23, against the Chicago Cubs, who were chasing the first-place Giants in the standings. The score was tied 1–1 with two outs in the ninth when the Giants' Moose McCormick walked. Merkle then singled, moving McCormick to third. When shortstop Al Bridwell followed with a single to score McCormick, Merkle—thrilled with his team's victory—simply headed toward the New York clubhouse in center field.

Johnny Evers, the Cubs's alert and peppery second baseman, noticed that Merkle hadn't touched second base, and he called for the ball. He wanted to touch second base, force Merkle, and prevent McCormick's run from counting. At this point, things began to get out of hand. The Giants, seeing what Evers had in mind, began yelling at Merkle to tag second, and he turned around and started for the base. The Cub outfielder who fielded Bridwell's hit tossed it toward Evers at second. By most accounts, Giant coach Iron Man Joe McGinnity intercepted the throw and was tackled by several Cubs, who tried to pry the ball away from him. Most reports have McGinnity finally heaving the ball deep into the left field stands.

Some observers swore that Merkle eventually touched the base, some claim he didn't. Some say Evers got another ball and stood on the base, appealing to the umpires, Bob Emslie and Hank O'Day. Fans and players were all over the field, shouting and arguing.

O'Day eventually agreed with Evers and the Cubs, called Merkle out, and declared the game a tie. The Cubs finished the season by winning eleven out of twelve to tie the Giants, so the two teams had to meet at season's end to replay the tie. The Cubs beat New York and Christy Mathewson 4–2, to take the National League pennant. The young Giant first baseman's mistake came to be known as the Merkle Boner.

John McGraw, far from being angry at Merkle, defended him constantly. What Merkle had done, he said, was done all the time by other players. Evers had just been smart enough to take advantage of it in a critical game. McGraw eventually made Merkle the Giants' regular first

Fred Merkle earned the nickname "Bonehead" for his historic baserunning blunder.

baseman, and even called him one of the game's smartest players. It made no difference. For the rest of his life, Fred Merkle was called Bonehead.

⚾ Why don't they use ⚾ aluminum bats in the big leagues?

Aluminum bats are a pretty new idea. And they're not a bad idea for kids' baseball, where replacing broken wooden bats can cost a lot of money. But you can hit a ball farther and faster with a metal bat than with a wooden one. So they turn fly balls into home runs, and they make hitters look better than they really are. If major league players were allowed to use them, every season batting record in the books would probably be broken. And more important, the added speed

of a ball lined out with an aluminum bat would provide a significantly higher chance of injury to infielders and, especially, pitchers. Besides, who wants to go to a big league game and hear *ping!* when Mark McGwire or Darrell Strawberry really gets hold of one?

Wooden bats were originally carved or turned on a lathe one at a time. They were so big that they rarely broke, and whole teams often shared just one or two of them. During the 1880s, Pete

Browning, a fine hitter who played with the Louisville team of the American Association, *did* break his bat. For a replacement, he went to a young wood-turner named Bud Hillerich. Browning liked his new bat so much that he talked it up among his teammates. Before he knew it, Hillerich was in the bat business, turning out for many players what he came to call Louisville Sluggers.

The heaviest bat used regularly during any season was Edd Roush's 48-ounce monster, though Babe Ruth is said to have used a 54-ounce model during spring training. The lightest were probably the 30-ouncers swung by Willie Keeler and Joe Morgan. The bats most big leaguers use today weigh between 32 and 34 ounces.

Wooden bats are made out of northern white ash. The companies that make them are more and more concerned about getting enough of the right kind of wood. At least one manufacturer is experimenting with graphite bats. The idea is to come up with something that sounds like wood, feels like wood, and hits the ball like wood, but which can be made of materials

Edd Roush wielded a 48-ounce bat.

that aren't running short. Who knows? Maybe in a few years, we'll be able to go to Little League or high-school games and not have to hear that awful *ping!*

⚾ *Are baseballs really made of horsehide?* ⚾

Not anymore, but official major league balls were covered with horsehide until it became too scarce in 1974. Now they are covered with cowhide.

From almost the earliest days of the National League, official NL balls were made by the A. G. Spalding Company. When the American League was founded in 1901, the A. J. Reach Company started making balls for that circuit, as it had for the American Association in the 1880s. Since Spalding owned Reach, it really made all the of-

ficial baseballs for the big leagues. The balls were manufactured in Chicopee, Massachusetts, and were stitched together by women—not by machines. In 1973, Spalding began making balls in Haiti, where they could hire workers to stitch the balls together much more cheaply. But a few years later, Spalding decided that—after almost a hundred years—it no longer wanted to manufacture baseballs for the big leagues. Rawlings now makes them for both leagues.

Early balls, before the major leagues

came into being, had rubber centers wound with yarn and covered with stitched leather. By the 1870s horsehide replaced cowhide, and in 1910, Spalding started using cork centers instead of rubber. In 1926, they started surrounding the cork center with cushioning material before winding on the thread. At various times, the type of thread has been changed, and so has the tightness with which the thread is wrapped. All of these changes changed the way the ball acted—usually making it more lively.

Back in the early '70s, Charlie Finley, who owned the Oakland A's, wanted the majors to begin using an orange ball. He thought it would be easier to see, and that it might add a little extra pizzazz to the game. The other owners didn't agree, and Finley's proposal went nowhere.

Al Spalding—great pitcher, club and league official, and baseball manufacturer.

What's the difference between interference and obstruction?

Easy. Interference occurs when a runner illegally tries to keep a fielder from making a play. Obstruction occurs when a fielder illegally tries to keep a runner from making his way around the bases.

The punishment for interference is for the batter (not the runner who interferes) to be called out. For obstruction, the umpire can award the runner a base.

Here's how an interference call might go. You're on first. The batter hits a perfect double-play ball to the second baseman, who tosses it to the shortstop as he crosses the bag. You are forced out at second, but you slam into the shortstop well off the base in an attempt to keep him from completing his throw to

first. Umpires often let this pass without an interference call, but if your ump is strict, he calls you for interference and declares the batter out. Double play the strange way.

Technically, when a catcher blocks the plate without the ball—a very common play these days—he is obstructing the runner. The umpire should award the runner home plate. Under the rules, a runner has an absolute right to a path to the base. A fielder is only supposed to be in the way if he's got the ball and is waiting to make the tag. Of course, if you're on base and a fielder grabs you as you begin to run, that's obstruction too. The umpire should award you the next base.

I manage to remember which of these

calls is which this way: Outside of baseball, an obstruction is usually something solid that doesn't move and is in your way—just like a fielder who's blocking a base illegally.

⚾ *Who was the slowest ballplayer?* ⚾

Just about all of baseball's famously slow runners were catchers, which makes sense. Catchers play the only defensive position that normally requires no running. They also play the one that takes the most out of the legs. *You* just try standing up and squatting down a hundred or more times a day every day all summer!

When I was a youngster, the man everybody called the slowest man in the majors was Gus Triandos, the Oriole catcher. Triandos had some power, and he made the American League All-Star team a couple of times. But he's probably best-known for trying to catch Hoyt Wilhelm's bobbing knuckleball. Manager Paul Richards finally designed a huge, hinged catcher's mitt to give Gus a little extra help. Rule makers soon declared that the mitt was too big, but a modified version is still used by catchers handling knuckleballers.

My grandfather lived in Cleveland

Ernie Lombardi was legendary for his slowness afoot.

during the teens. I remember him laughing as he told me stories about how slow Steve O'Neill, the Indian catcher in those days, was. He claimed to have seen O'Neill hit a ball that went through a hole in the fence at old League Park. But O'Neill didn't know it had gone through, and he staggered all the way around the bases as fast as he could go, and all but collapsed at the plate. Grampie always said that O'Neill had been so slow that he made Triandos look like a sprinter.

Probably the slowest of all, though, was big Ernie Lombardi, the Hall of Fame catcher for the Reds during the '30s and early '40s. Lombardi was big— 6'3' and 230 pounds—and he ran flat-footed. Pitcher Kirbe Higbe said, "I could run faster with a mule on my back than Ernie." The amazing thing about Lombardi was that he was a good enough hitter to have led the league twice in batting. You can bet he did it without beating out any infield grounders!

⚾ Why aren't there any ⚾ lefthanded-throwing catchers?

Actually, it's more a matter of tradition than anything else. Jack Clements played 17 years in the big leagues as a lefthanded catcher (1884–1900), but he was by far the most successful. The original idea seems to have been that lefthanded catchers would have more trouble throwing to second base than righthanded catchers. Why? Because there are more righthanded hitters than lefties, and they'd get in the way of a lefthanded catcher's arm as he stood up to fire the ball.

This is true as far as it goes. There *are* more righties than lefties, and a batter on the same side of the plate as your throwing arm *can* get in your way a little when you throw. But big league catchers—all righthanded throwers—are still expected to get the ball to second base in a hurry and on the money when a lefthanded batter is up. And when they don't, it usually has nothing to do with the hitter being in the way. Lefthanded catchers? Let 'em play! (But good luck finding a mitt!)

Jack Clements was a fine lefthanded catcher in the nineteenth-century.

You almost never see lefthanded second basemen, third basemen, and shortstops. The reason is that for a lefty to make a throw to first from any of these positions, he has to pivot his entire body instead of making just a single step.

On the other hand, some people have argued that a lefthanded shortstop could reach more balls in the hole because his glove would be to that side. And the same would be true of a third baseman handling balls up the line. Lefty Mike Squires played a little third base for the White Sox a few years ago and looked pretty good, and Don Mattingly of the Yankees made some fine plays when he stepped over there temporarily in 1985. Years ago, Wee Willie Keeler filled in quite often at third base, and Hal Chase played 36 games at second base.

Most people, though, aren't convinced. Making that throw to first is tough enough when you're naturally set up for it. Having to take an extra step might give a lot of hitters infield hits.

And a lefthanded second baseman has even more problems. Imagine trying to make the pivot on a double play: You'd probably have to spin all the way around toward the outfield before you could get your throw off!

Being a lefty, though, is a real advantage to a first baseman. His glove is on the side of his body where balls are most likely to be hit. And in most situations, he's in a better position to hold a runner on first and make a quick tag when the pitcher throws over.

So if you're lefthanded and you want to play the infield, get yourself a mitt and work out around first base. It's probably going to be your only shot.

A few baseball nicknames are so well known that we almost forget they're nicknames. Babe Ruth, for example. His real name was George Herman Ruth. He was still a boy in his teens when Jack Dunn, the owner of the then minor league Baltimore Orioles, acquired him for the team. The other players began calling him Jack's Babe, and the game's most famous nickname was born.

Actually, Ruth was called Jidge by his teammates on the Red Sox, and at least during his early years on the Yankees. "Jidge" was just "George" said in a phony New England accent.

Ruth himself, by the way, had a terrible time remembering other people's names. He called almost everybody "Kid."

Lots of great players were given nicknames by newspaper writers, but these names were never used by teammates. Ty Cobb was the Georgia Peach, Honus Wagner was the Flying Dutchman, Christy Mathewson was Big Six, and Walter Johnson was the Big Train. In later years, Joe DiMaggio was the Yankee Clipper, and Ted Williams was the Splendid Splinter.

In baseball's earliest days, there were even more flowery nicknames given to players by newspaper writers. Bob Ferguson played for a number of big league teams from 1871 through 1884. He was so famous for his fielding ability that he was called Death to Flying Things Ferguson in the papers. Something tells me that his teammates probably stuck to Bob.

My favorite nickname of the nineteenth century is actually a very simple one: Dirty Jack Doyle. Doyle played for a number of teams between 1889 and 1905. I've never been able to find out what he was really like, but the name makes him sound like a pirate—and he never even played for Pittsburgh!

Shoeless Joe Jackson supposedly got his nickname when he took his new spikes off in the outfield one day because they were hurting his feet. The nickname stuck, though, because he was a poorly educated Southern boy, and Shoeless Joe made him sound like the hillbilly many Northern sportswriters took him to be.

There once was a pitcher named Walter Beck. He labored on and off for several bad teams from 1924 through 1945. Walter never had much success, while batters facing him seemed to do quite well. If you look in the *Baseball Encyclopedia* today, you won't find Walter Beck listed in the heavy print. But you will find Boom-Boom Beck. There's some dispute about whether the *booms* are supposed to represent the sound of bat hitting ball or ball hitting outfield fence. But there's no doubt Walter earned them either way.

Before Boom-Boom Beck there was Baby Doll Jacobson. And before Baby Doll Jacobson there was Piano Legs

Bob Ferguson was so adept at snaring line drives that he earned the colorful nickname "Death to Flying Things."

Hickman. Just take a look through any good book of individual records and you'll find dozens of wonderful and amazing baseball nicknames. You're sure to come up with your own special favorites.

⚾ Who's the greatest ⚾ home run hitter of all time?

That's easy—or is it? In the major leagues, Hank Aaron hit more—755—than anyone. So he must be the best. But wait a minute. Roger Maris hit 61 in one season. Nobody else has done that, so he must be the best. Hold on, though. Babe Ruth hit homers more *often* than any American player—one every 11.8 official at-bats—so the Babe must be the man.

This gets a little complicated. Let's ease off for a minute and take a look at other great home run performances over the years. Way back in 1884, a Chicago White Stocking third baseman named Ned Williamson hit 27 homers. This was an amazing total at the time—almost three times higher than anyone had ever hit before.

But Williamson set his record in Lake

Hank Aaron's 715th home run in Atlanta Stadium, April 8, 1974.

Front Park, one of the smallest ballparks of all time. The distances down the lines were only 180 and 190 feet. The White Stockings played in Lake Front Park for two years. The first year, balls hit over those short fences were ground-rule doubles. In 1884, they were called home runs, and Williamson obviously had the right stroke to take advantage of the change. In 1885, Chicago moved into another park. Williamson never again hit more than eight homers in a season.

The greatest home run hitter before Ruth was really Roger Connor, a big first baseman for the New York Giants. He hit 136 over an 18-year career. He led the league only once, but he consistently racked up totals over 10—heavy power in those days. An interesting thing about Connor is that he is still fifth on the all-time list for triples. So he not only pounded the ball, but he had enough speed to get around the bases pretty quickly too.

Fifty years later, another National League player demonstrated some consistent power. From 1946 through 1952, Ralph Kiner led the league in home runs seven times in a row (he twice shared the top spot with Johnny Mize). Over that span, Kiner hit a homer for every 12.8 official at-bats. And he hit over 50 twice. Babe Ruth and Mickey Mantle are the only other two men to do that.

A few years later in the American League, Harmon Killebrew was winning home run championships from 1959 right through 1969. He won or shared six titles over that span and had yearly totals in the forties six times.

Since then, Mike Schmidt has been the most impressive home run producer. He's led the National League eight times since 1974. Schmidt's yearly totals don't compare with those of Kiner or Killebrew, but his productive career has been longer. And while he's been belting the ball out of parks, he's also been one of the game's premier defensive third basemen.

Okay, enough of this. Back to the original question. Who was the greatest home run hitter of all time? Let's look at it this way: Who would you bet on to win a home run hitting contest among all these guys in their prime? I'd bet on the Babe, myself. But I wouldn't bet too much.

Has a rookie ever been the batting champ?

Only once in each league. Peter Reiser batted .343 to lead the National League in 1941, his first full year with Brooklyn. Reiser was a great hitter, a terrific baserunner, and a wonderful outfielder. But he had a very short career because he kept running into walls. He was very badly injured a number of times, and he was only a part-time player by 1948. Many baseball people think Pistol Pete could have been one of the all-time greats.

Tony Oliva had played a few games for the Minnesota Twins in 1962 and 1963, but he was still officially a rookie in 1964, when he led the league with a .323. He proved it was no fluke by taking the title again the next year with a .321 average. In 1971, he came back to do it again: .337. Oliva's career was cut short by injuries too. He became a designated hitter and retired after the 1976 season.

Ty Cobb hit only .240 in his first year up with the Tigers. Two years later, though, he hit .350 at the age of twenty to win his first title. For almost fifty years, he remained the youngest man ever to do that. His mark was broken by another Tiger, Al Kaline, who was a few days younger when he took the American League batting title with a .340 in 1955.

In 1975, Fred Lynn of the Red Sox may have had the best all-around rookie season anyone has ever had. He was brilliant in center field, and he hit .331 with 21 homers and 105 RBIs. He was named both Rookie of the Year and Most Valuable Player—the only time that's ever been done. A few years later, Lynn won his batting title, hitting .333 in 1979.

Joe Jackson might have had the toughest luck of any great rookie. In 1911, he hit .408—the highest any first-year player ever registered. He didn't win the title, though. Cobb hit .420!

Fred Lynn, then of the Red Sox, who in 1975 may have had the best all-around rookie season in recent memory.

⚾ Have there always been ⚾ four balls and three strikes?

Even people who know nothing about baseball are usually aware that it's "one, two, three strikes, you're out," and that you take your base on four pitches out of the strike zone.

These have been the rules for a full century. But back in the early days, there was a lot of fiddling around. Three strikes usually meant an out (in some years there was a "warning pitch" if the batter failed to swing at a good pitch), but before 1889, it would have taken more than four bad pitches to send you down to first.

In the 1870s, a batter was allowed to call for the ball where he wanted it: high or low. A pitcher had *nine* chances to put the ball in the proper strike zone. In 1880, the number of balls was changed to eight. And the number required for a walk kept going down: to seven in 1881, to six in 1884, to five in 1886.

In 1887, the rules were changed so that a batter could no longer call for a high or low ball. It still took five balls to walk, but for this year only, a walk was counted as a hit. The result was some very high batting averages—Tip O'Neill of the St. Louis Browns led the league at .492!

There was another strange change of the rules in 1887. If a batter took a called third strike, he got one more chance to hit. In effect, this gave batters four strikes much of the time.

The next year, 1888, rules were

89

changed again. Walks were no longer counted as hits. And baseball went back to the three-strikes-and-you're-out rule. Finally, in 1889, things settled down.

Rule makers decided on four balls for a walk, and that's the way it's been ever since.

⚾ *Which team in baseball history* ⚾ *had the most Hall of Fame players?*

The New York Yankees in 1930, 1931, 1932, and 1933 had eight players on the roster who would wind up in the Baseball Hall of Fame. All four squads had Babe Ruth, Lou Gehrig, center fielder Earle Combs, catcher Bill Dickey, and pitchers Red Ruffing, Herb Pennock, and Lefty Gomez. The 1930 club also had pitcher Waite Hoyt, and in 1931, 1932, and 1933 the team had third baseman Joe Sewell.

The interesting thing about these four Yankee clubs is that only one of them won the pennant. They were third in 1930, behind the Philadelphia A's and the Washington Senators. In 1931, they were second to the A's. In 1933, the Senators beat them to the wire. They did take the flag in 1932, when they went on to sweep the Chicago Cubs four straight in the World Series.

The great Yankee team of 1927—often considered the best of all time—had "only" five future Hall of Famers on the

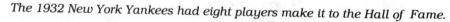

The 1932 New York Yankees had eight players make it to the Hall of Fame.

roster: Ruth, Gehrig, Combs, Hoyt, and Pennock.

That same year, the Yankees' rivals across the river, the New York Giants, had seven future Hall of Famers in the clubhouse. The Giants finished only third. Actually, the Giants roster showed seven future Hall of Famers six times during the '20s. But they won just two National League pennants.

Why don't teams full of great players win everything in sight? Well, partly because they sometimes run up against other teams full of great players. From 1929 through 1931, for example, the Yankees were up against the powerful Philadelphia A's, who had five future Hall of Famers on their own rosters.

Sometimes, too, the great names on the rosters are too young or too old to contribute much. On that 1927 Giant team, for example, Mel Ott was just an eighteen-year-old kid. He played only 32 games in the outfield that year. He later went on to hit 511 major league home runs.

Most important, though, is the fact that baseball is a team game. The vital thing is not just how well players play but how well they play *with each other*.

Has a big league ballplayer ever been killed in a game?

Yes. In August 1920, Cleveland shortstop Ray Chapman was beaned by pitcher Carl Mays of the Yankees, and he died the next day. It remains major league baseball's greatest tragedy.

Mays was a very good pitcher. He ended the 1920 season with a 26–11 record. He was righthanded and used a submarine motion, something like Dan Quisenberry uses today. Mays was also a very tough cookie. He had a reputation for throwing close to batters—even at them sometimes. Because of his submarine motion, Mays's fastball tended to move in on righthanded batters like Chapman.

In 1920, umpires kept the same ball in play as long as possible. So Chapman was looking at a dirty, scuffed ball coming at him out of Mays's strange delivery. He never really moved to get out of the way, so he may not have picked up the flight of the ball until it was too late. In those days, players did not wear batting helmets, and the pitch hit Chapman flush on the temple.

Soon after Chapman's death, umpires were instructed to take discolored balls out of play.

Ray Chapman was an excellent shortstop on an excellent team. Cleveland went on that year to win both the American League pennant and the World Series against Brooklyn. Writer Bill James has said that Chapman probably would have been elected to the Hall of Fame if he'd had the chance to play out his career.

Carl Mays might have made the Hall of Fame too. He pitched for another decade and ended his career with a record of 208–126, for an outstanding winning percentage of .623. But he wasn't a likable man, and many people thought that he didn't seem sorry enough that his pitch had killed another player. There were always suspicions that the rough and tough Mays

The only on-field death in major-league history—Carl Mays (right) threw the unfortunate pitch; Ray Chapman (left) was struck by it.

had actually been throwing at Chapman. No one will ever know for sure.

Since 1920, beanings have shortened the careers of players like Mickey Cochrane, Ducky Medwick, Tony Conigliaro, and Dickie Thon. But no other big leaguer, thank goodness, has ever been killed on the field.

⚾ *Which team has finished last the most times?* ⚾

Poor Philadelphia! The two least successful franchises over the years have both lost most of their games representing the City of Brotherly Love.

The Phillies have finished last in the National League 24 times, starting in 1883. The Phils won a pennant in 1915, and they have been a pretty good team through most of the 1970s and '80s. But they ran up long strings of cellar finishes during the '20s, '30s, and '40s. They won a pennant with the Whiz Kids in 1950, but by the end of that decade, they were putting together four more last-place seasons. In 1961, they lost 23 games in a row to set a National League record. Their most recent finish at the bottom of the barrel was in 1972. They finally won their first—and only—World Series championship in 1980.

The other big Philadelphia losers are the Athletics, who later moved on to Kansas City and then Oakland. They've managed to finish last twenty-four times too. But they've done it in fewer years. The A's didn't first land in the cellar until 1915. But once they wound up there, they didn't get out for seven years—an all-time record. The Philadelphia A's finished last three times in the '30s, six times in the '40s, and twice in the '50s. Then they moved to Kansas City and did it six more times through the '50s and '60s. As the Oakland A's, they've managed to stay out of the cellar.

The interesting thing about the Athletics is that they've also put together several of the greatest teams in the history of the game. Under manager Connie Mack, Philadelphia won four pennants in five years from 1910 through 1914. This was the team of the famous $100,000 Infield of Stuffy McIn-nis at first, Eddie Collins at second, Frank "Home Run" Baker at third, and Jack Barry at shortstop. At the end of 1914, Mack broke that great team up, and it took him more than a decade to put another powerhouse together. When he did, players like Jimmie Fox, Al Simmons, Mickey Cochrane, and Lefty Grove tore the American League apart. They won three straight pennants from 1929 through 1931.

Years later, in Oakland, the A's of Reggie Jackson, Joe Rudi, Catfish Hunter, and Vida Blue took three straight World Series championships during the early '70s.

So the Phillies and Athletics have shown that even the worst teams don't have to stay that way.

⚾ What's the most runs ever ⚾ scored in a big league game?

Way back in 1897, Chicago beat Louisville in a National League game, 36–7. Neither team was especially good that year. Chicago finished ninth in the twelve-team league. Louisville finished eleventh. A reserve outfielder on that bad Louisville club was the great Honus Wagner, later to become one of the game's best shortstops with the Pittsburgh Pirates.

Since 1900, the most runs any team has managed in a game is 29. It's happened twice, both times in the American League. In 1950, a strong Boston Red Sox team beat the weak St. Louis Browns, 29–4. In 1955, the Chicago White Sox defeated the Kansas City Athletics, 29–6.

In the National League, the record since 1900 was set by the St. Louis Cardinals, who beat the Philadelphia Phillies 28–7. The Cards really weren't that much better than the Phils. They finished fourth, while Philadelphia finished fifth.

Sometimes two teams both hit like crazy in the same game. On August 25, 1922, the Chicago Cubs beat the Phillies 26–23. The 49 runs scored in the game remains an all-time record. How would you have liked being a pitcher that day?

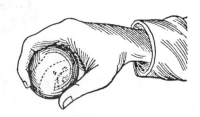

I read about pitcher's "scuffing" balls so they can throw tricky pitches. How do you make a scuffed ball break?

Well, you don't—if you're playing by the rules. Up until 1920, almost anything went. Pitchers used to spit on or grease balls. They scratched them or roughed them up. And it was all legal. In 1920, "trick" pitches like this were banned. The pitcher could make the ball spin, or,

in the case of the knuckleball, not spin, all he wanted to. But he could no longer put anything on the ball, or do anything to the ball's cover.

Of course, many pitchers have continued—illegally—to throw both spitters and scuffballs.

Ed Walsh threw a great spitball, winning 40 games in 1908.

The idea behind both kinds of pitches is simple. For a spitter, the pitcher wets (or greases up) his index and middle fingers, then throws the ball with his normal motion. The ball slips off those two fingers and picks up a reverse spin from his thumb. The result is a pitch that breaks sharply downward. This sounds simple, but there have actually only been a few pitchers who really threw the pitch well. The greatest was probably Ed Walsh, a Hall of Famer for the Chicago White Sox who won 40 games in 1908.

For a scuffball, the pitcher makes a cut, scratch, or rough spot on the ball. He usually does this in one of the two areas where the stitches are farthest apart. Then he throws the ball with the abraded side facing either to the right or to the left. Because the cut changes the way air flows around the ball as it comes to the plate, the ball breaks in the direction away from the scuff.

A pitcher throwing illegal pitches like this usually scuffs the ball himself. Sometimes, though, the catcher cuts the ball on part of his equipment. Pitchers have used everything from sandpaper to emery boards to thumbtacks to sharpened belt buckles.

Today, few great pitchers make illegal pitches a major part of their games. They have enough success with their fastballs, curves, sliders, and change-ups. Although there are exceptions, the guy who throws a lot of spitters or scuffballs is usually a pitcher who realizes he needs a special edge if he wants to stay in the big leagues.